New Directions for
Student Services

John H. Schuh
EDITOR-IN-CHIEF

Elizabeth J. Whitt
ASSOCIATE EDITOR

Serving Native American Students

Mary Jo Tippeconnic Fox
Shelly C. Lowe
George S. McClellan
EDITORS

Number 109 • Spring 2005
Jossey-Bass
San Francisco

SERVING NATIVE AMERICAN STUDENTS
Mary Jo Tippeconnic Fox, Shelly C. Lowe, and George S. McClellan (eds.)
New Directions for Student Services, no. 109
John H. Schuh, Editor-in-Chief
Elizabeth J. Whitt, Associate Editor

NEW DIRECTIONS FOR STUDENT SERVICES (ISSN 0164-7970, e-ISSN 1536-0695) is part of The Jossey-Bass Higher and Adult Education Series and is published quarterly by Wiley Subscription Services, Inc., A Wiley Company, at Jossey-Bass, 989 Market Street, San Francisco, California 94103-1741. Periodicals Postage Paid at San Francisco, California, and at additional mailing offices. POSTMASTER: Send address changes to New Directions for Student Services, Jossey-Bass, 989 Market Street, San Francisco, California 94103-1741.

New Directions for Student Services is indexed in College Student Personnel Abstracts and Contents Pages in Education.

Microfilm copies of issues and articles are available in 16mm and 35mm, as well as microfiche in 105mm, through University Microfilms Inc., 300 North Zeeb Road, Ann Arbor, Michigan 48106-1346.

SUBSCRIPTIONS cost $75 for individuals and $170 for institutions, agencies, and libraries. See ordering information page at end of book.

EDITORIAL CORRESPONDENCE should be sent to the Editor-in-Chief, John H. Schuh, N 243 Lagomarcino Hall, Iowa State University, Ames, Iowa 50011.

www.josseybass.com

Contents

PREFACE

This is a volume that you should read, think about, and share with your colleagues. Few resources are available to help us understand the Native American student experience in higher education. This volume will be a great addition to that literature, helping us broaden our understanding of Native American culture, Native American sovereignty, and the Native American student experience.

Why is such an understanding important? After all, Native American students are a small segment of the student population in the vast majority of U.S. colleges and universities. Why should you as a professional in higher education invest in learning about the unique circumstances, needs, hopes, dreams, and aspirations of students who are Native American?

Learning about the Native American student experience is important for a number of reasons. First, as educators, we should be committed to dispelling stereotypes and learning the truth about the experience of all of our students. Many of our ideas about the Native American experience are based on perceptions gleaned from movies, the popular fiction or press, and stories we heard when we were children. Because we have not been exposed to information about the reality of contemporary Native American educational experiences, those stereotypes tend to shape our attitudes and reactions to the few Native American students on our campuses. When we do not check facts, dispel stereotypes, learn about difference, and appreciate new perspectives, we are teaching powerful negative lessons to the students we serve.

Second, as professionals in higher education, we must understand the diverse and complex nature of the Native American experience in higher education in the United States. There is a reason that the editors of this volume have provided tribal designations for the Native American authors contributing to this volume: all the authors bring unique cultural experiences to their writing and the perspectives that they share with the reader. Appreciating the diverse nature of the Native American experience is a critical step toward increasing understanding of this population within our student bodies.

Third, the information and perspectives provided in this volume will help us think in new ways about our definitions of multiculturalism, pluralism, and inclusion. Our own experiences, our own interactions, and our own knowledge base often limit our views of diversity. Most campuses (the exception being those with larger Native American populations) have not included Native American students in their planning, programs, structures, and organizations. The authors in this volume will help broaden your views of multiculturalism and inclusion.

Finally, it makes good sense to broaden our own personal and professional perspectives and range of understanding about the complex web of human relationships that make up the higher education enterprise. When we do so, we become better administrators, teachers, professionals, and role models.

An old saying states "What you don't know won't hurt you, so leave well enough alone." In this instance I could not disagree more strongly. I believe that lack of knowledge about Native American students can hurt those students in both seen and unseen ways. It will also certainly hurt non-Native American students if we do not take the lead in increasing their understanding about the unique factors that shape the Native American student experience. Lack of knowledge about Native American students and Native American people can hurt us as professionals and limit our effectiveness. I urge you to read this volume carefully and to use it as a springboard to increasing your own base of knowledge of the Native American experience on the contemporary U.S. college campus.

DR. MARGARET J. BARR *is professor emeritus and former vice president for student affairs at Northwestern University.*

EDITORS' NOTES

This volume is intended to serve as a sourcebook and a source of conversation for several audiences. We hope that the information and insights in this volume will prove useful to those who are seeking ways to better serve Native American students in tribally controlled colleges and universities or at predominantly white institutions of higher education, as well as those who are helping Native American students to prepare themselves for postsecondary education. In addition, the volume may serve as a resource for students and faculty in graduate preparation programs or Native American studies programs who are interested in this area of higher education for which little other literature is available. Tribal educators, tribal leaders, and Native American students and parents might also find this volume helpful in providing a better understanding of how colleges and universities, particularly predominantly white institutions, organize their services and pursue their institutional goals.

The value of knowledge about Native American people and a Native American worldview extends beyond providing an informed base for practice in serving Native American students. The study of indigenous epistemologies, cultural traditions, and social structures also provides a richer array of options through which everyone can seek to understand and address the problems and opportunities that challenge them in the broad scope of their work and their lives.

In focusing on Native American students in higher education, the goal of this volume is not to essentialize Native American identity or experience. Being Native American is one aspect in a compounding, contradicting, and complex set of identities and experiences that contributes to the uniqueness of individual Native American people. Native American identity and experiences are, however, an important aspect that the scholarship of student affairs and higher education has too long overlooked.

Through the preface by Margaret J. Barr and the prayer by Henrietta Mann (Cheyenne), the volume opens with the voices of elders. The next two chapters provide a broad overview of information that will be helpful to the reader while moving through the volume. Chapter One presents a brief history of Native American higher education in the United States. In Chapter Two James A. Larimore (Comanche) and George S. McClellan present a discussion of Native American student success in U.S. higher education. The next three chapters present various Native American perspectives in higher education. Shelly C. Lowe (Navajo) describes student experiences in Chapter Three. Raymond D. Austin (Navajo) offers insights into the perspectives of tribal leaders and parents in Chapter Four. In Chapter Five Mary Jo

Tippeconnic Fox (Comanche) discusses the experiences of Native American staff and faculty (as well as the role that Native American and non-Native staff and faculty play in the success of students who are Native American). Perry G. Horse (Kiowa) discusses Native American identity in Chapter Six, followed in Chapter Seven by Gregory A. Cajete's (Tewa) essay on indigenous epistemology. The next two chapters address working with Native American students in different types of institutions. In Chapter Eight Robert G. Martin (Cherokee) describes the work of tribally controlled colleges and universities. Donna L. Brown (Turtle Mountain Chippewa) shares information in Chapter Nine about the American Indian student services program at the University of North Dakota as one model of serving Native American students at a predominantly white institution. The volume closes with some parting thoughts from the editors in Chapter Ten.

A goal of this volume is to provide an opportunity for Native American voices to be heard, but we acknowledge that the editing process does not lend itself to conveying fully the power of Native American voices. We are grateful to the contributing authors of this volume; their combined voices are its strength. Thanks to John Schuh and Liz Whitt for seeing a volume on serving Native American students as being important and for their help in preparing this volume for publication. Thanks also to Peggy Barr and Ruth Harper for their willingness to serve as readers along the way. In addition, we appreciate the financial support received from the NASPA Foundation for a project that served as the catalyst for this volume. Finally, we are grateful to our friends, colleagues, and families for their support throughout the development of this volume. Whatever success this volume has in achieving its goals is the result of the contributions of all these people. Any shortcomings are ours and ours alone.

Mary Jo Tippeconnic Fox
Shelly C. Lowe
George S. McClellan
Editors

DR. MARY JO TIPPECONNIC FOX *(Comanche) is chair of American Indian Studies and ambassador to the Indian nations at the University of Arizona.*

SHELLY C. LOWE *(Navajo) is a doctoral candidate in higher education at the University of Arizona.*

DR. GEORGE S. MCCLELLAN *is vice president for student development at Dickinson State University*

PRAYER

Creator of the wonders and mysteries of life,
We thank you for your gifts of the mind, sight, hearing, motion, and speech.
In the beginning, just as our beloved ancestors thanked you for your abundant blessings, we too thank you for the blessings we enjoy today.

With your awesome power, you gave your humble children of earth the breath of life from the winds of the east, south, west, and north.
As we journey on earth, the gentle breezes and mighty winds remind us of your power and enduring love for your entire creation contained within the sacred circle.
We cannot live without Earth's breath of life that we know as air that flows and blows from the four directions.
In infinite holiness you connected breathing and air with sound and with life.
With sacred air we make our thoughts manifest in the sounds of words, song, and language.

With your awesome power, you gave your humble children of earth the gift of the mind.
As we journey on earth, the inner human thoughts of our minds remind us of your power and enduring love for your entire creation contained within the sacred circle.
In blessing us with the mind, you intended us to develop it in respectful and useful ways.
In blessing us with the mind, you intended that we become educated about life and for life.
You instructed that we balance thinking with the mind with the thinking of the heart, so that we can be loving, compassionate human beings respectfully walking on earth.
In infinite holiness you connected our minds and hearts with that of the spirit.

Today and for tomorrow, I ask blessings upon those who have written this book.
Continue to bless them with good hearts, great minds, and strong spirits.
I ask your blessings upon their thoughts and words that appear on the leaves of the tree of life.
They are concerned for the education of those who are young to the earth journey or who have yet to come to this miracle place called earth.

Know them for their good words that are balanced with thinking with their
   hearts.
Know them for their wisdom and understanding.
Know them for their strong spirit-filled lives.
With the sacred breath of life, I thank you for their words and lives.

I ask that the teachings contained within this book be useful.
I also ask blessings upon each of those who touch this book, who open this
   book, who read this book, and who hear it with the voice of the heart.
Neaese! Thank you.
As we move through time, I ask that we continue to honor your creation
   and that the world be filled with the goodness of peace for today and all
   time that is to be.

DR. HENRIETTA MANN (CHEYENNE) *is the Endowed Chair in Native American*
Studies at Montana State University, Bozeman. She also serves as a member of
the Council of Elders for the American Indian Science and Engineering Society
and as a member of the board of trustees for the National Museum of the Amer-
ican Indian at the Smithsonian Institution.

This chapter provides an overview of the three eras in the history of Native American higher education in the United States: the colonial, federal, and self-determination eras.

Where We Have Been: A History of Native American Higher Education

George S. McClellan, Mary Jo Tippeconnic Fox (Comanche), and Shelly C. Lowe (Navajo)

Although the literature has paid attention to certain aspects of Native American education in the United States, it has largely not addressed Native American higher education. Writing in the early 1990s, Tierney (1992, p. 1) noted, "Native Americans are one of the smallest ethnic minorities of the United States population, and American Indian students are among the most underrepresented groups in academe. In part because of both of these factors, there is little research about Native American undergraduate experiences in higher education."

The waning of the twentieth century and dawn of the twenty-first century have brought little change with respect to the extent to which the literature addresses Native American higher education (Carney, 1999; McClellan, 2003).

Drawing on the extant literature, this chapter provides an overview of Native American higher education. The overview begins by explicating the constructed definition of several important terms used in the chapter and throughout this volume. Using the framework of three eras, the chapter then presents an overview of the history of Native American higher education in the United States.

Constructed Definitions

The term *Native American* as used in this chapter and throughout the volume refers to people who identify as Native American, Alaska Native, or Native Hawaiian. The term *minority* is used here in the way that it is commonly used in higher education, referring to people who are members of an ethnic minority. It is important to be mindful that tribal affiliation is far more powerful for many Native Americans than is identification with the broader pan-Native construct (Horse, 2001) and that one extension of the idea of Native American tribal sovereignty is that Native Americans are a political minority rather than an ethnic minority.

The term *tribal sovereignty* is a complex social and legal construction (American Indian Higher Education Consortium [AIHEC], 2000). As used in this volume, the term includes the recognition of Indian nations and the right of those nations to enact and enforce their own laws. It also refers to the right of Native American people to self-determination in all matters pertaining to their lives.

Drawing on the work of Lomawaima (1999), the term *Native American higher education* throughout this work has three meanings. First, it refers to the experiences of people who are Native American in European American institutions of higher education. Second, the term refers to the experiences of people who are Native American in tribally controlled institutions of higher education. Finally, the term is used to reference the broader construct of tribally controlled colleges and universities.

Three Eras in Native American Higher Education

In developing an understanding of the history of Native American higher education in the United States, it is important to have in mind the broader context of the history of Native American people in this country. As Cabrera (1978, p. 158) notes, "American Indians are victims of a legacy which includes economic exploitation, military conquest, political manipulation, and social disregard." Education, including higher education, has been part and parcel of the development of that legacy (DeJong, 1993; Szasz, 1999).

The history of Native American higher education in the United States may be understood as consisting of three eras: colonial, federal, and self-determination (AIHEC, 2000; Carney, 1999). This chapter briefly describes each of the three eras.

Colonial Era. The colonial era of Native American higher education began with the first contact between Europeans and Native American people and extending to the Revolutionary War (AIHEC, 2000; Carney, 1999). Although three of the nine original colonial colleges included educating Native Americans in their original statements of purpose or mission, these early colleges did little to provide higher education for Native Americans. During their combined eighty years of operation between their founding and the American Revolution, Harvard University, the College of William and Mary, and Dartmouth College enrolled only forty-seven Native American students, only four of whom graduated (Carney, 1999). With respect to their espoused mission to educate Native Americans, the colonial colleges failed utterly (AIHEC, 2000; Belgarde, 1996; Wright, 1996).

What accounts for this failure? One reason may be that the founders of colonial colleges were more interested in the appeal of a mission of educating Native Americans in fundraising than they were in actually advancing the education of Native American students (Carney, 1999).

Another reason for the failure might be that Native Americans saw Euro-American higher education as having nothing of value to offer them. Those who took part were not welcomed into colonial society, and other Native American people viewed them skeptically when they returned to their tribal communities (AIHEC, 2000). Indeed, there are several reports of tribal leaders politely declining offers to send Native American young men to colonial institutions of higher education because of the perception that such experiences resulted in a lessening of important traditional skills without a concomitant gain in new skills of value in tribal life (AIHEC, 2000; Noriega, 1992; Thelin, 2003).

Lomawaima (1999, p. 5) describes the goal of colonial colleges in educating Native Americans this way: "to transform Indian people and societies and eradicate Indian self-government, self-determination, and self-education." More than simple lack of interest, the failure of colonial colleges and universities to educate Native Americans may reflect many Native Americans' resistance to assimilation through Euro-American higher education (AIHEC, 2000).

Federal Era. The federal era of Native American higher education began with the development of treaty relationships between the United States government and Native American nations following the American Revolution and extending through the advent of the movement toward Native American self-determination (AIHEC, 2000; Carney, 1999). Ninety-seven treaties addressing education for Native Americans were signed between 1778 and 1871 (Belgarde, 1996), and the United States government created a trustee responsibility for Native American education as a matter of these treaty obligations and subsequent legislation. The government signed the first treaty with a provision for higher education in September 1830 with the Choctaw Nation. The treaty provided for scholarship funds, but those funds were not used until 1841, when Choctaw students attended white institutions (Olivas, 1996).

Despite the boom in college development in the United States in the late 1800s and early 1900s (including the development of higher education institutions for women and African Americans), Native American higher education was overlooked. Most of the activity that took place during this time involved religiously affiliated academies (AIHEC, 2000), a number of which later abandoned or minimized their mission to educate Native Americans (for example, Ottawa University in Kansas or University of Tulsa). At the beginning of the twentieth century, only two colleges focused on Native American higher education (Carney, 1999): Sheldon Jackson College, founded in 1878 to educate Alaskan Natives (Olivas, 1996), and Croaton Normal School, the only state-supported four-year institution for

Native Americans until the midtwentieth century (University of North Carolina, Pembroke, 2004).

Although the Meriam Report of 1928 (a report prepared for the Department of the Interior critical of earlier U.S. policy regarding Native American issues) did suggest that Native Americans should be encouraged to participate in higher education (AIHEC, 2000), the federal era is notable for its lack of activity in the area of Native American higher education and the predominant focus on postsecondary vocational education. The education services that the U.S. government provided for Native Americans during the federal era were driven by the same objectives that drove similar efforts in colonial institutions: Christianization, forced acculturation, and assimilation (Belgarde, 1996).

Self-Determination Era. Although scholars differ about when the self-determination era began, there is little doubt that the Progessive movement in education and the passage of the Indian Reorganization Act in 1934 are watershed moments in the era and pivotal events in the movement toward Native American self-determination in education (AIHEC, 2000; Carney, 1999). Its emphasis on vocational education notwithstanding, the Progressive movement is notable in the history of Native American education for appreciating Native American culture and insisting that the curriculum bring in the culture rather suppressing or eradicating it (AIHEC, 2000). The Indian Reorganization Act of 1934 affirmed Native American sovereignty and self-determination with regard to education and included the first federally designated scholarship funds for Native American higher education (Carney, 1999).

Challenges of Termination. Whereas Carney (1999) uses the passage of the Indian Reorganization Act (and the Johnson-O'Malley Act) in 1934 to mark the beginning of the era of self-determination, AIHEC (2000) uses the initial activity in the development of tribally controlled colleges in the late 1960s instead. The latter view reflects the varying degrees of indifference and hostility that characterized the relationship between the federal government and Native Americans during the intervening decades. Throughout the 1940s and 1950s, the federal government sought to terminate its trust relationship with Native Americans, relocate Native Americans from reservations by incentive (as contrasted with earlier federal efforts to use force to put Native American people on reservations), and shift responsibility for Native American services to the states. Pursuit of the termination policy had disastrous consequences for Native American people (Boyer, 1997b). Many tribes were removed from the roll of those recognized by the federal government, and substantial numbers of Native Americans relocated to pan-Native enclaves in urban areas such as Chicago, Cleveland, and Oakland (Belgarde, 1996).

From the 1930s to the 1960s. The federal focus in Native American postsecondary education remained for the most part on vocational training (AIHEC, 2000). Some Native American soldiers returning from service in

World War II made use of the GI bill to enter college, and the Bureau of Indian Affairs implemented a scholarship program of its own in 1948. About the same time, tribal support for college scholarships increased as well. Szasz (1999, p. 114) has referred to this increasing tribal support for higher education as "one of the most promising developments" during the era. Despite the increased availability of funding, there was very modest growth in Native American enrollment in higher education from the 1940s through the 1960s: enrollment in higher education hovered around two thousand students in the late 1950s and reached only thirty-five hundred students by the late 1960s (AIHEC, 2000; Carney, 1999).

Opposition from non-Natives as well as from reservation and urban Native Americans led the government to back away from termination and relocation in the 1960s. In its place the federal government began to pursue policies of self-determination for Native Americans (Boyer, 1997b). Key pieces of federal legislation related to Native American self-determination with respect to education include the Indian Education Act of 1972, the Indian Self-Determination and Assistance Act of 1975, and the Education Amendments of 1978 (Belgarde, 1996).

Tribally Controlled Colleges and Universities

The single most significant development in the era of self-determination in Native American higher education, however, has been the emergence of the tribal college movement (AIHEC, 2000; Carney, 1999; Stein, 1999). The Cherokee developed the first tribally controlled schools (one male seminary and one female seminary) in the 1850s, but both disintegrated following the passage of the Curtis Act in 1898, which abolished tribal governments and led to federal control of the Cherokee Nation's education system (AIHEC, 2000; Belgarde, 1996). The first tribally controlled community college (then the Navajo Community College, now Diné College) was founded in 1968 (Belgarde, 1996).

The passage of the Navajo Community College Act of 1971, the Indian Education Act of 1972, the Indian Self-Determination Act of 1975, the Tribally Controlled Community College Act of 1978, and the extension of the Morrill Act to tribal colleges in 1994 have helped to foster the growth in the number of tribally controlled colleges since the 1960s (AIHEC, 2000; Carney, 1999; Stein, 1999). The United States now has thirty-four tribally controlled colleges (a thirty-fifth college exists in Canada near the U.S. border).

Tribally controlled colleges and universities must be chartered by a tribe and typically have an all–Native American board that is independent of the tribal government in order to insulate the institution from tribal politics. The president is typically Native American, but the faculty is often primarily non-Native. Tribal elders frequently serve as instructors and advisers at the institution (Belgarde, 1996). Most of the tribally controlled institutions of higher education offer associate degrees; six offer bachelor's degrees (Sinte Gleska University, Oglala Lakota College, Salish Kootenai College, Haskell Indian Nations University, Nazarene Bible College, and American Indian College); and two (Sinte Gleske and Oglala Lakota) offer master's degrees (Carney, 1999).

According to Belgarde (1996, p. 9), tribally controlled colleges and universities "promote the culture of the tribe they serve, work to strengthen the economies of their Indian communities, and strengthen the social fabric of the tribal community both internally and in conjunction with outside communities through empowering individual Indian people." Tribally controlled institutions are typically located on a reservation and serve students who live on or near that reservation. Student bodies at tribally controlled colleges and universities are on average older than their peers at mainstream institutions, are predominantly women (often with children), have very low income levels, and are first generation (Belgarde, 1996). With respect to individual students, "Tribal colleges act as a bridge between Indian students and the outside world. Often, they help the Indian student who is 'stopping-out' from a majority, society college re-enroll by providing emotional, academic, and financial support and assistance. Or, the college might provide specific training to equip students for particular job opportunities becoming available off the reservation, but within commuting distance" (p. 9).

Given the role of tribally controlled colleges in the lives of Native American communities and Native American students, it is not surprising that some refer to these colleges as "islands of hope" (DeJong, 1993, p. 244). A national study of students in tribally controlled colleges (Boyer, 1997a) reveals a tremendous level of engagement in and satisfaction with those institutions. Graduation rates in tribally controlled colleges are similar to those of mainstream community colleges, and several studies show that individuals who attend tribally controlled institutions benefit in both employment and wages (Boyer, 1997b). These results provide support for the contention that "perhaps the singular story of the late twentieth-century Indian higher education lay in the rise and expansion of the tribally controlled colleges" (Szasz, 1999, pp. 234–235).

Tribally controlled colleges and universities, however, face some unique challenges in the new millennium. Tensions exist between the purposes of preserving tribal culture and promoting tribal economic development; further tensions exist between Native American and non-Native professionals working in and with these institutions (Belgarde, 1996). Many tribally controlled institutions struggle with insufficient or deteriorating facilities (Boyer, 1997b). An ongoing and significant challenge to tribally controlled colleges and universities is a lack of adequate funding. Olivas (1996) points out that the current difficult financial climate in higher education, a source of concern even for majority institutions, is particularly threatening to minority institutions given the relative lack of public support for minority issues. There are structural impediments to funding such as accreditation requirements for federal funding. Such impediments were in part the reason that only seven of twenty-five awards for Native American programs made in 1979 under Title III (Strengthening Developing Institutions) went to tribally controlled colleges and universities while the remainder went to mainstream institutions (Olivas, 1996). Similarly, according to Stein (1999), the original allocation of $5,280 per Native American student (full-time equivalent) that the Tribal College Act of 1983 provided would have to have been $8,450 in 1998 to keep pace with the consumer price index. The actual allocation that year was a mere $2,900 per student. The mid-1990s were a new low point in federal funding for Native American higher education, with tribally controlled colleges receiving less than half of the funds promised (Szasz, 1999).

Non-Native Colleges and Universities

There have also been healthy and important developments in Native American higher education at non-Native institutions since the late 1960s. In addition to the tribally controlled colleges and universities, three private religiously affiliated institutions focus on Native American higher education (Bacone College, Nazarene Indian Bible College, and American Indian College), and three federally controlled institutions focus on Native American higher education (Haskell Indian Nations University, Southwestern Indian Polytechnic Institute, and the Institute for American Indian Art) (AIHEC, 2000).

At eighty-five non-Native institutions, Native Americans are more than 5 percent of the enrollment. It is important to note, however, that only seven of those institutions enroll more than five hundred Native American students. In fact, including tribally controlled colleges, only three institutions enroll more than one thousand Native American students (Carney, 1999).

Native American Studies

Not only have there been gains in Native American enrollment in higher education, but academic institutions have developed numerous programs in Native American studies since the 1960s. Currently, nearly one hundred and thirty Native American studies programs exist at colleges or universities in Canada and the United States (Nelson, 2004). Kidwell (1999, p. 271) observes that the development and persistence of these programs in college curricula "has both contributed to and been made possible by a growing body of scholarship that encompasses key themes of tribal sovereignty, cultural integrity, relationship with the land, and importance of Native languages for American Indian communities."

Summary

It is impossible to calculate the cost to Native Americans and non-Native Americans of the lack of any meaningful effort in Native American higher education for the first more than two hundred years of our shared history. "With a truly effective educational structure contributing to a maximum exchange of knowledge and awareness between the two cultures, what might have been realized?" (AIHEC, 2000, p. 137).

However one understands the reasons for the lack of attention to Native American higher education in the past, it is important to recognize our shared future (Pavel, 1999). To realize our potential in this regard, we must resolve to further our understanding of the history of Native American higher education and strengthen our commitment to Native American students.

References

American Indian Higher Education Consortium (AIHEC). *Creating Role Models for Change: A Survey of Tribal College Graduates.* Washington, D.C.: AIHEC, 2000. http://www.aihec.org/rolemodels.pdf. Accessed June 8, 2003.

Belgarde, W. L. "History of American Indian Community Colleges." In C. Turner, M. Garcia, A. Nora, and L. I. Rendón (eds.), *Racial and Ethnic Diversity in Higher Education* (ASHE Reader Series). Boston: Pearson Custom Publishing, 1996.

Boyer, P. "First Survey of Tribal College Students Reveals Attitudes." *Tribal College Journal,* 1997a, 9(2), 36–41.

Boyer, P. *Native American Colleges: Progress and Prospects.* Princeton, N.J.: Carnegie Foundation for the Advancement of Teaching, 1997b.

Cabrera, V. A. *Minorities in Higher Education: Chicanos and Others.* Niwot, Colo.: Sierra, 1978.

Carney, C. M. *Native American Higher Education in the United States.* New Brunswick, N.J.: Transaction, 1999.

DeJong, D. H. *Promises of the Past: A History of Indian Education.* Golden, Colo.: Fulcrum, 1993.

Horse, P. G. "Reflections on American Indian Identity." In C. L. Wijeyesinghe and B. W. Jackson III (eds.), *New Perspectives on Racial Identity Development: A Theoretical and Practical Anthology.* New York: New York University Press, 2001.

Kidwell, C. S. "The Vanishing Indian Reappears in the College Curriculum." In K. G. Swisher and J. W. Tippeconnic III (eds.), *Next Steps: Research and Practice to Advance Indian Education.* Charleston, W.V.: ERIC Clearinghouse on Rural Education and Small Schools, 1999.

Lomawaima, K. T. "The Unnatural History of American Indian Education." In K. G. Swisher and J. W. Tippeconnic III (eds.), *Next Steps: Research and Practice to Advance Indian Education.* Charleston, W.V.: ERIC Clearinghouse on Rural Education and Small Schools, 1999.

McClellan, G. S. "Multiculturalism as a 'Technology of Othering': An Exploratory Study of the Social Construction of Native Americans by Student Affairs Professionals in the Southwest." Doctoral dissertation, University of Arizona, 2003. Abstract in *Dissertation Abstracts International,* 64, 05A.

Nelson, R. M. *A Guide to Native American Studies Programs in the United States and Canada.* http://oncampus.richmond.edu/faculty/ASAIL/guide/guide1.html. Accessed Dec. 27, 2004.

Noriega, J. "American Indian Education in the United States: Indoctrination for Subordination to Colonialism." In M. A. Jaimes (ed.), *The State of Native America: Genocide, Colonization, and Resistance.* Boston: South End Press, 1992.

Olivas, M. A. "Indian, Chicano, and Puerto Rican Colleges: Status and Issues." In C. Turner, M. Garcia, A. Nora, and L. I. Rendón (eds.), *Racial and Ethnic Diversity in Higher Education* (ASHE Reader Series). Boston: Pearson Custom Publishing, 1996.

Pavel, D. M. "American Indians and Alaska Natives in Higher Education: Promoting Access and Achievement." In K. G. Swisher and J. W. Tippeconnic III (eds.), *Next Steps: Research and Practice to Advance Indian Education.* Charleston, W.V.: ERIC Clearinghouse on Rural Education and Small Schools, 1999.

Stein, W. J. "Tribal Colleges: 1968–1998." In K. G. Swisher and J. W. Tippeconnic III (eds.), *Next Steps: Research and Practice to Advance Indian Education.* Charleston, W.V.: ERIC Clearinghouse on Rural Education and Small Schools, 1999.

Szasz, M. C. *Education and the American Indian: The Road to Self-Determination Since 1928.* (3rd ed.) Albuquerque: University of New Mexico Press, 1999.

Thelin, J. R. "Historical Overview of American Higher Education." In S. R. Komives and D. B. Woodard (eds.), *Student Services: A Handbook for the Profession.* (4th ed.) San Francisco: Jossey-Bass, 2003.

Tierney, W. G. *Official Encouragement, Institutional Discouragement: Minorities in Academe—The Native American Experience.* Norwood, N.J.: Ablex, 1992.

University of North Carolina, Pembroke. "History of UNCP." http://www.uncp.edu/uncp/about/history.htm. Accessed Dec. 27, 2004.

Wright, B. "The 'Untameable Savage Spirit': American Indians in Colonial Colleges." In C. Turner, M. Garcia, A. Nora, and L. I. Rendón (eds.), *Racial and Ethnic Diversity in Higher Education* (ASHE Reader Series). Boston: Pearson Custom Publishing, 1996.

DR. GEORGE S. MCCLELLAN *is vice president for student development at Dickinson State University.*

DR. MARY JO TIPPECONNIC FOX (COMANCHE) *is chair of the American Indian studies program and ambassador to the Indian nations at the University of Arizona.*

SHELLY C. LOWE (NAVAJO) *is a doctoral candidate in higher education at the University of Arizona.*

2

This chapter surveys the literature on Native American student retention, framing the discussion in the context of the broader body of literature on retention.

Native American Student Retention in U.S. Postsecondary Education

James A. Larimore (Comanche), George S. McClellan

Attrition, persistence, and *retention* are among the terms or labels common in discussions about a troubling phenomenon in U.S. postsecondary education: many more students enter colleges and universities than graduate with degrees. Although the disparity between rates of initial enrollment and rates of graduation exists for all student populations, the gap is greatest among students who are African American, Hispanic, or Native American (National Center for Education Statistics, 2002).

The problem of underrepresentation among those earning degrees is particularly acute for Native American students (Benjamin, Chambers, and Reiterman, 1993). Although precise retention data is difficult to obtain for a number of reasons (Boyer, 1997b; Carney, 1999), estimates of attrition rates for Native American students in higher education range from between 75 percent to 93 percent (Brown and Robinson Kurpius, 1997). For many (though certainly not all) Native American students, leaving college prior to completion of a degree signals delayed or foregone personal aspirations and often diminished or deferred opportunities. But the departure of these students also has a detrimental impact on their campus communities because their absence diminishes the cross-cultural educational potential of the learning and living environment for all.

This chapter surveys the higher education literature on Native American student retention, framing the discussion in the context of the broader body of literature on retention. The chapter begins with exploring the link between retention of Native American students in higher education to both secondary persistence rates and rates of postsecondary participation.

It then provides an overview of the literature on Native American student retention. The chapter concludes with recommendations for both practice and research.

Secondary Persistence and Postsecondary Participation

The literature on postsecondary retention of Native American students is situated within the broader context of both the literature on persistence in secondary education and the literature on rates of participation in postsecondary education.

The problem of retention does not begin with college enrollment. According to the American Council on Education (2002), 8 percent of whites, 15 percent of African Americans, and 28 percent of Hispanics drop out of high school. The situation for Native American high school students is even more dire. Tierney (1992b) reported that more than 40 percent of Native American students who entered secondary education nationwide left without a high school diploma.

According to Neisler (1992), fully 60 percent of all students who graduated from high school in 1989 immediately enrolled in college. In contrast, Tierney (1992b) cited several studies indicating that only 40 percent of the Native American students who graduate from high school will enroll in postsecondary education.

Native American Student Retention

The severe underrepresentation of Native Americans among those earning degrees reflects both extremely low enrollment or participation rates and generally poor retention rates for Native American college students. McEvans and Astin (as cited by Pavel, 1992) identify Native Americans as among the least likely to enroll in public four-year institutions and the least likely to persist to graduation in those institutions. Both Astin (1982) and Tierney (1992b) discuss the low retention rates for Native American students. Although Tierney notes the complex problems associated with determining a precise figure, he reports that the retention rate for Native American students may be as low as 15 percent overall.

Even though the attrition of Native American college students is a noted fact, much uncertainty remains about the factors and forces that influence students' decisions to persist with college. This uncertainty stems from the general dearth of research on the higher education experiences of American Indians (Falk and Aitken, 1984; Tijerina and Biemer, 1988; Wright, 1985), the insufficient representation of Native Americans in national and longitudinal research databases (Benjamin, Chambers, and Reiterman, 1993; Pavel and Padilla, 1993), and the scarcity of studies that take into account students' tribal and cultural backgrounds as possible factors related to persistence

(Belgarde, 1992; Benjamin, Chambers, and Reiterman, 1993; Murguia, Padilla, and Pavel, 1991; Pavel and Padilla, 1993; Tierney, 1991; Wright, 1990, 1991).

Application of Euro-American Theories of Retention. A number of scholars have addressed Native American student retention in higher education through theoretical frameworks developed without regard to ethnicity or frameworks that used Euro-Americans as the primary reference group for the initial construction of the theory. Despite the criticism of his work by Tierney (1992a), Tinto's theory of student departure (1975, 1986) continues to serve as the point of departure for numerous studies of Native American student retention (for example, Brown, 1995; Brown and Robinson Kurpius, 1997; Cain, 1997; Mayo, Murguia, and Padilla, 1995; Pavel and Padilla, 1993). Others have used Pace's work (1982) on the quality of student effort as the basis for their studies (for example, Castellanos, Kuh, and Pavel, 1998; Cole and Denzine, 2002).

Application of Indigenous-Based Theories of Retention. An emerging body of scholarship makes use of indigenous-based perspectives or theories in addressing Native American student retention. Dodd, Garcia, Meccage, and Nelson (1995) provide a rare example of a qualitative study focused on Native American students who persisted in higher education published in a mainstream journal. Though not exclusively focused on retention, Garrod and Larimore (1997) present one of the most extensive qualitative studies of the Native American student experience, providing a collection of personal narratives from Native Americans who attended Dartmouth College. Similarly, though using a quantitative methodology, Boyer (1997a) reported the results of the first national study of the experiences of Native American students enrolled in tribally controlled institutions of higher education.

Indigenous-based theoretical frameworks for addressing retention of Native American students are also emerging. As an example, Heavyrunner (Heavyrunner and DeCelles, 2002; Heavyrunner and Morris, 1997) has applied resiliency theory (Clark, 2002) to the question of Native American persistence in higher education using the Family Education Model, an indigenous-based approach to addressing Native American retention in education.

Individual Factors in Student Persistence. Several studies have identified support from family, supportive staff and faculty, institutional commitment, personal commitment, and connections to homeland and culture as key factors in the persistence of Native American students (Dodd, Garcia, Meccage, and Nelson, 1995; Falk and Aitken, 1984; Jackson and Smith, 2001; Reyhner and Dodd, 1995; Rindone, 1988). These same studies identified a number of obstacles to retention and graduation for Native American students, including inadequate academic preparation, vague constructs of educational or vocational goals, financial aid, discrepancies between high school and college environments, prejudice, and social isolation. Importantly, these studies also found that many Native American students stopped out of their educational pursuits for a period of time at least once along the way to completing their degree. Tierney (1991) noted that some factors viewed as critical to Native American student retention (for example, lack of academic preparation or loneliness) should be understood as common to students from all backgrounds, whereas other factors (for example, the need to return home for ceremonies or the potential conflict between Western science and traditional ways of knowing) are unique to students who are Native American.

Social and academic integration are the focus of several studies from the interactionist perspective. Social integration, particularly formal social integration into campus life as evidenced by active participation in campus groups or the establishment of meaningful social networks, appeared to be positively correlated to academic performance for Native American students (Cain, 1997; Mayo, Murguia, and Padilla, 1995). However, there are indications that the rate of return with respect to the impact of social effort on academic success is not as great for Native American students as it is for white students (Castellanos, Kuh, and Pavel, 1998). The work of Cibik and Chambers (1991) and Hornett (1989) emphasized the role of the institution and its faculty in promoting academic integration among Native American students. With respect to quality of effort, no significant differences appear between the quality of either academic or social effort of Native American and white students (Castellanos, Kuh, and Pavel, 1998; Cole and Denzine, 2002).

Precollege academic preparation is the focus of another cluster of articles on Native American student retention. Brown (1995) found that academic preparation and aspirations prior to college and academic performance in college were most highly correlated with Native American student persistence, a finding consistent with the earlier work of Patton and Eddington (1973). Beaty and Beaty (1986) noted what they described as institutional cultural impediments to Native American student academic success but argued that the responsibility for addressing these impediments rests with the students rather than with both the student and the institution.

Cultural Identity and Persistence. The nexus of cultural identity and persistence is a frequent subject in the literature of Native American student retention and one that is changing considerably. Early articles (for example, Boutwell, Low, Williams, and Proffit, 1973; Carroll, 1978; United States Office of Education, 1965) posited a view of cultural identity that was zero sum in nature. These articles argued that Native American students had to choose between achieving academic success through assimilation into the majority culture or maintaining their traditional culture at the expense of their educational goals.

Recent articles present a decidedly more complex framework, suggesting that cultural identity and resistance to assimilation are important matters in understanding the social and academic integration experiences of

Native American college students (Belgarde, 1992; Hornett, 1989; Pavel and Padilla, 1993; Tierney, 1991; Tijerina and Biemer, 1988; Wright, 1985, 1990, 1991). Several of these studies see students as able to operate (or being challenged by operating) simultaneously in both the majority culture of higher education and their own traditional culture (Benjamin, Chambers, and Reiterman, 1993; Huffman, Sill, and Brokenleg, 1986; Rindone, 1988; Scott, 1986; Whitehorse, 1992). Wright (1985, 1990, 1991) viewed the experiences of today's Native American college students as a continuation of the struggle of Native American people to succeed in education on their own terms—achieving mastery and maintaining a strong cultural identity while resisting assimilation.

Huffman's use (2001) of resistance theory and the transculturation hypothesis to discuss the role of cultural identity in the departure or persistence decision offers a particularly promising path for future exploration in this area. His work, along with the work of others mentioned in this section, suggests that Native American students who are able to draw strength from their cultural identity while adapting to the demands of campus life are more likely to succeed in their academic pursuits than are either culturally assimilated students or those unable to establish a level of comfort within their campus environment.

Role of Perceived Racism and Stress. Several studies of Native American student retention have focused on the impact of student perceptions of the campus climate or campus culture. Locust (1988) described the ways in which cultural differences might lead to misunderstanding and contribute to student departure. Huffman (1991) and Perry (2002) both found that significant percentages of Native American students experienced generalized verbal racism or harassment on predominantly white campuses. Belgarde (1992) found that perceptions of hostility or racism were significantly higher for students with a stronger sense of Native American cultural identity. Lin, LaCounte, and Eder (1988) found that students' attitudes toward college and feelings of isolation are significantly correlated to college academic performance as measured by grade point average.

Belgarde (1992), Edgewater (1981), and Peregoy (1990) explored the more general issue of Native American student stress. Heinrich, Corbine, and Thomas (1990) discussed techniques for use in counseling Native American students. Among their recommendations for counselors are to expect expressions of anger, use culturally appropriate metaphors, and consider suggesting the use of a vision quest if appropriate to the student's tribal culture.

Specific Native American Populations. Relatively few studies about the retention of Native American students have focused on students from specific tribes. Jackson and Smith's study (2001) of Navajo student transitions to postsecondary education and Kleinfeld and Kahout's work (1974) on improving retention rates among students who are Alaska Natives are two examples of such studies. Similarly, Kidwell's study (1976) is a rare example of work focused specifically on Native American women in higher education.

Kidwell (1986, 1989) also discussed low enrollment and retention of Native American students in graduate and professional education. Buckley's ethnographic study (1997) of eight graduate and professional students and Tate and Schwartz's study (1993) of retention among Native American students enrolled in a nursing degree program are two more examples of the relatively few studies in this area.

Institutional Factors in Student Persistence. Student decisions concerning college persistence represent the outcome of a complex longitudinal process of interaction between an array of individual and institutional factors. Although an individual student's background characteristics may influence and shape that person's initial educational intentions and commitments, scholars believe that students' college experiences play a more substantial role in their integration into the academic and social systems of the college. However, as Wright (1985) suggests, American Indian college students may present unique academic, social, cultural, and psychological needs as they attempt to establish themselves in the academic and social systems of a campus.

Student Retention in Tribally Controlled Colleges. Several studies have documented that retention rates for Native American students enrolled at tribal colleges are higher than those for Native American students enrolled at mainstream institutions (Laden, Millem, and Crowson, 2000). Boyer (1997a, 1997b) described the successful outcomes (that is, employment, transfer rates, and continued studies) for many tribal college students but also noted the challenges that those institutions face with respect to student retention. Despite these challenges, Laden, Millem, and Crowson (2000) described tribal colleges as positive, albeit atypical, examples among all institutions of higher education based on their performance with respect to student retention.

Role of Finances in Native American Student Retention. Almeida (1999) identified lack of adequate family financial resources (and consequently a complete reliance on financial aid), bureaucratic and paperwork hurdles, unrealistic student earning requirements, unacknowledged costs, and distrust of officials as potential obstacles to Native American student enrollment and persistence in higher education. Earlier studies by Dodd, Garcia, Meccage, and Nelson (1995), Falk and Aitken (1984), and Reyhner and Dodd (1995) provide a foundation for Almeida's position. Tierney (1992b) noted in his multi-institutional qualitative study that family socioeconomic background did not have as great a role in predicting Native American persistence as it did for whites, even though Native American students generally came from lower socioeconomic backgrounds than their white peers. These studies suggest that the composition of financial aid packages as well as the total award and other factors warrant closer scrutiny in understanding Native American persistence.

Role of Staff and Faculty. Several studies have noted positive out-comes associated with involvement in the campus Native American community, including contact with American faculty and staff (Belgarde, 1992; Falk and Aitken, 1984; Wright, 1985). Tierney (1991) noted the dearth of Native American staff and faculty in higher education and argued that non-Native staff and faculty must orient themselves to the concerns and issues of Native American students. Brown and Robinson Kurpius (1997) concurred, advocating that non-Native staff and faculty must play a key role in shaping campus environments that are welcoming, supportive, and affirming of students who are Native American. Discussing the role of faculty (both Native American and non-Native) in the retention of Native American students, Hornett (1989, p. 12) asserted that faculty "are the persons who can most directly affect the motivation and desire of Indian students to remain in school." A considerable amount of research has documented the value of formal and informal faculty contact on learning and other educational outcomes (Hornett, 1989; Loo and Rolison, 1986; Pascarella, 1985; Pascarella and Terenzini, 1991; Stoecker, Pascarella, and Wolfle, 1988).

Retention Programs for Native American Students. A number of studies have identified student services as being especially important in the persistence of Native American students (for example, Cibik and Chambers, 1991; Jenkins, 1999; Lin, LaCounte, and Eder, 1988; Pavel and Padilla, 1993; Wright, 1985). Several studies have reported a possible connection between the lack of institutional support systems or the lack of satisfaction with available systems with a weakening of educational goals and commitments for Native American students (Benjamin, Chambers, and Reiterman, 1993; Falk and Aitken, 1984; Lin, LaCounte, and Eder, 1988; Murguia, Padilla, and Pavel, 1991; Pavel and Padilla, 1993; Rindone, 1988).

Belgarde (1992) found that participation in Stanford University's American Indian program mediated the process of academic and social engagement for Native American students. The works of Beaty and Beaty (1986) and Osborne and Cranney (1985) are typical of other articles focused on local support programs to help institutions retain Native American students.

Kleinfeld, Cooper, and Kyle (1987) outlined a program of counseling in secondary education that was designed to promote Alaska Native participation in and persistence through postsecondary education. Similarly, Shutiva (2001) argued that culturally sensitive academic and career guidance programs are needed in secondary education. Brown and Robinson Kurpius (1997) suggested that a proactive and somewhat intrusive academic advising program for first-year students was an important means of improving persistence among Native American students.

Cross (1993) offered a study of Native American student services centers at a cross section of public and private four-year institutions. Carney (1999) provided recommendations for the development of support programs based on his review of the literature. Among the recommendations were "a much expanded recruitment program extending to the family as well as the student, and to those out of high school for a few years; a much more elaborate socialization and orientation program; attention to monitoring of progress and ongoing support; the development of Native American faculty; and job experience by the students" (pp. 146–147).

Issues in Research Methodology. As with all academic research, the studies referenced in this chapter have limitations based on the researchers' methodologies. Most of the studies reviewed here focused on relatively small numbers of students who attended a single institution rather than larger populations or random samples drawn from larger populations. These studies benefit from consideration of the local or campus context and offer helpful information about the student experience in those settings, but this affects the generalizability of the findings to other settings. Readers should note these limitations but should not use them to dismiss or diminish the important contributions found in the work.

The current state of the available research points out the critical need for additional study. Further, given the urgent need to improve the participation, persistence, and graduation of Native American college students, additional resources should be directed to this area of inquiry. As a matter of shared interest to tribal and other governmental agencies, foundations, individual campuses, and state educational systems, this area would benefit from a coordinated and comprehensive research effort aimed at improving campus practices and programs.

Recommendations for Practice

The literature on Native American student retention reveals a complex situation that involves the elaborate interplay of individual characteristics and actions on the one hand and institutional factors on the other. As we noted earlier in this chapter, students' academic preparation and initial educational intentions influence and shape the way they approach college. Therefore, practitioners in higher education would be wise to stay abreast of the changing experiences of the secondary students who each year become college students. As Burr, Burr, and Novak (1999) noted, we must consider Native American student retention in secondary schools and higher education as related parts of a seamless whole.

Although precollege experiences are undeniably important, the available literature indicates that students' experiences once they are enrolled in college play a substantially larger role in their successful integration into the academic and social environments of the campus. College students have access to a wide variety of support services, including extensive orientation experiences, academic advising, counseling, financial aid, and so on. In spite of the availability of such services, it is sometimes difficult for students to access the right services at the time they most need them. For example, a problem with financial aid might delay the acquisition of textbooks and cause a student to fall seriously behind in her courses. Not surprisingly, students who encounter such situations often have a hard time getting caught up in their course work and find themselves at risk for academic probation or suspension. Such situations point out that the student who encounters difficulty in one part of the college experience often faces challenges in other areas as well.

It is not uncommon for the same student to simultaneously require advice about course selection, time management and study skills, financial aid, the possible diagnosis of a learning disability, and other personal concerns. Unfortunately, on many campuses it is quite possible that no single staff member will have a holistic understanding of the student's total situation—or how best to coordinate the services available to support the student. One of the difficult truths is that although campuses provide a wide array of support services, many do not do an effective job of coordinating the delivery of multiple services to the same student. The end result can be poor coordination or worse, an environment in which students simply slip through the cracks and terminate their studies.

Although student services offices sometimes operate as functional silos, containing valuable resources but only loosely connected to other programs that serve the same students, the good news is that this condition is amenable to change. Our experience in student services leads us to believe that what is needed is an institutional instigator or catalyst to cultivate a more coordinated and comprehensive approach to retaining Native American students. Such an approach exists on a number of campuses, but colleges and universities can do more to share information about effective models and strategies.

Admissions counselors, coordinators of orientation programs and advising, financial aid advisers, and representatives from residential life, student health staff, and other support personnel should meet periodically to discuss how they can work together in better serving Native American students. Staff in programs focused on leadership development, mentoring, and undergraduate research opportunities should also be involved, as the overall goal is not just retention but the enhancement of the educational experience. The purpose of these meetings should be to share or pool information about the general experiences of Native American students and to develop case management teams to help individual students resolve those issues that require coordination between different offices or programs. By extension, the meetings should serve as a reminder that each office or program shares in the responsibility to improve retention and the overall educational experience for Native American students.

Staff should share openly in such meetings information about retention and graduation rates, course completion rates for gateway courses in various fields of study, academic performance in required first-year courses, and use and satisfaction rates for support services (and other available measures).

The focus of the examination and discussion of such information should be identifying strengths as well as areas of shared concern and a commitment to collaborative efforts to improve awareness of services or effectiveness of services for Native American students. Though the potential for misunderstanding and distrust might be significant at the outset, there is no better way to improve the effectiveness of campus support services than through open and constructive dialogue between practitioners who share a commitment to students.

The literature on Native American student retention suggests the potential benefits of using multiple theoretical lenses or perspectives to enhance our understanding and to develop a shared storehouse of ideas and concepts. King (2001) offers four factors that affect educational achievement for minority students: representation, climate and intergroup relations, education and scholarship, and institutional transformation. With the addition of financial aid and financial resources to these four dimensions, a more useful conceptual framework begins to emerge for understanding the factors that affect Native American student persistence in higher education. When we add cultural identity and resiliency, the framework improves further.

Swail and Holmes (2000) present a five-part integrated minority student retention framework that makes a solid point of departure for institutional planning related to Native American student retention: recruitment and admissions, financial aid, academic services, student services, and curriculum and instruction. Academic institutions might integrate the work of King (2001), Swail and Holmes (2000), and Kirkness and Barnhardt's four Rs (respect, relevance, reciprocity, and responsibility) (1991) to develop a culturally rooted and culturally responsive plan for enhancing success for students who are Native American.

Additional exploration is clearly needed in the area of financial aid policy, especially to the forms of aid as well as the amounts of aid available (Turner, 2001). Those on campus concerned with the issue of Native American student retention, including student affairs professionals, need to inform themselves better about the impact of financial aid and financing policy.

Although staff and faculty need to take personal responsibility to understand the issues that Native American students face, institutions must be committed to collaborating with Native American students, their families and tribes, and other resources if they are to become places where the goal of Native American student success is the "mastery of developmental tasks, rather than a simple counting of student enrollment or a recording of grades" (Wright, 1987, p. 18). An example of such an approach would be for institutions to provide office space on campus for tribal educators and tribal leaders so that they could continue to provide support to Native American students and so that the institution could benefit from their expertise.

Recommendations for Research

There is a clear need for additional scholarly research on the experiences of Native American students in postsecondary education. Scholars have done valuable work to date; and new developments, such as the work on cultural identity and resilience and other approaches rooted in indigenous perspectives, are promising. The following areas offer promise to researchers interested in informing future efforts to improve Native American student retention in colleges and universities:

Revising Tinto's theory of student departure (1975, 1986) or developing new alternatives to it (Braxton, 2000).

Advancing the work under way on alternative constructs and conceptual frameworks; Huffman's work (2001) on resistance theory and the transculturation hypothesis and the work of Heavyrunner and others on resilience and the Family Education Model are among the promising alternative frameworks in need of further exploration.

Developing research projects that allow for comparative analysis across several institutions in addition to analysis within particular institutions.

Adding to the existing, albeit sparse, body of qualitative work on the experiences of Native American students in postsecondary education (see, for example, Garrod and Larimore, 1997).

Developing a culturally based model of identity development for Native American people.

Exploring the experiences, perspectives, and needs of Native American faculty and staff in postsecondary institutions, particularly with respect to their interactions with students who are Native American.

Examining the factors that have influenced the creation and development of support programs for Native American students.

Swisher and Tippeconnic (1999) suggest that an important next step in addressing the problems in Native American higher education is for Native American researchers to focus their attentions and efforts in this area. This will require institutions to educate and graduate greater numbers of Native American scholars and reconsider the marginalization of ethnic studies.

Research on Native American higher education, however, should not be the sole responsibility of Native American scholars, just as Native American student retention cannot be the sole responsibility of Native American students, staff, and faculty. Non-Native scholars from a variety of disciplinary backgrounds must become engaged in research in this multidisciplinary field as well. In doing so, non-Native researchers must first recognize that they, like all other people, have their own biases (for example, gender, ethnicity, culture) and should seek out ways to conduct research that is culturally sensitive and Native-centered. An important mutual step forward would involve partnerships between non-Native scholars and Native American scholars, tribal leaders, and other Native American people who can provide cultural and other insights and on occasion admonitions about the experience of conducting research in Native American higher education.

Conclusion

This chapter has presented a review of the literature on Native American retention in postsecondary education, which is but one aspect of the complex and evolving world of Native American education. The available literature indicates that scholars have made progress in understanding this complicated topic, but there is clearly still a great deal yet to do.

References

Almeida, D. A. *Postsecondary Financial Aid for American Indians and Alaska Natives.* Charleston, W.V.: ERIC Clearinghouse on Rural Education and Small Schools, 1999. (EDORC 993)

Astin, A. W. *Minorities in American Higher Education: Final Report of the Commission on the Higher Education of Minorities.* San Francisco: Jossey-Bass, 1982.

Beaty, J., and Beaty, C. K. "University Preparation for Native American Students: Theory and Application." *Journal of American Indian Education,* 1986, 26(1), 6–13.

Belgarde, M. J. "The Performance and Persistence of American Indian Undergraduate Students at Stanford University." Doctoral dissertation, Stanford University, 1992. Abstract in *Dissertation Abstracts International, 53,* 05A.

Benjamin, D., Chambers, S., and Reiterman, G. "A Focus on American Indian College Persistence." *Journal of American Indian Education,* 1993, 32(2), 24–40.

Boutwell, R. C., Low, W. C., Williams, K., and Proffit, T. "Red Apples." *Journal of American Indian Education,* 1973, 12(2), 11–14.

Boyer, P. "First Survey of Tribal College Students Reveals Attitudes." *Tribal College Journal,* 1997a, 9(2), 36–41.

Boyer, P. *Native American Colleges: Progress and Prospects.* Princeton, N.J.: Carnegie Foundation for the Advancement of Teaching, 1997b.

Braxton, J. M. (ed.). *Reworking the Student Departure Puzzle.* Nashville, Tenn.: Vanderbilt University Press, 2000.

Brown, L. L. "Psychosocial Factors Influencing the Academic Persistence of American Indian College Students." Doctoral dissertation, Arizona State University, 1995. Abstract in *Dissertation Abstracts International, 55,* 04A.

Brown, L. L., and Robinson Kurpius, S. E. "Psychosocial Factors Influencing Academic Persistence of American Indian College Students." *Journal of College Student Development,* 1997, 38(1), 3–12.

Buckley, A. "Threads of Nations: American Indian Graduate and Professional Students." 1997. (ED 444 771) http://www.eric.ed.gov.

Burr, P. L., Burr, R. M., and Novak, L. F. "Student Retention Is More Complicated Than Merely Keeping the Students You Have Today: Toward a 'Seamless Retention Theory.'" Abstract in *Journal of College Student Retention,* 1999, 1, 239–253.

Cain, C. L. "Becoming Members of the Academic Community." Unpublished master's thesis, Arizona State University, 1997.

Carney, C. M. *Native American Higher Education in the United States.* New Brunswick, N.J.: Transaction, 1999.

Carroll, R. E. "Academic Performance and Cultural Marginality." *Journal of American Indian Education,* 1978, 18(1), 11–16.

Castellanos, J., Kuh, G., and Pavel, M. "American Indian and Alaska Native Students and the Student Involvement Model." Paper presented at the 23rd Association for the Study of Higher Education conference in Miami, Fla., Nov. 1998.

Cibik, M. A., and Chambers, S. L. "Similarities and Differences Among Native Americans, Hispanics, Blacks, and Anglos." *NASPA Journal,* 1991, 28(2), 129–139.

Clark, A. S. *Social and Emotional Distress Among American Indian and Alaska Native Students: Research Findings* (ERIC Digest). Charleston, W.V.: ERIC Clearinghouse on Rural Education and Small Schools, 2002. (ED 459 988)

Cole, J. S., and Denzine, G. M. "Comparing the Academic Engagement of American Indian and White College Students." *Journal of American Indian Education,* 2002, 41(1), 19–34.

Cross, S. L. "A Cross-Sectional Study of Selected Four-Year Public and Private Colleges in the United States with American Indian (Native American) Student Support Programs." Doctoral dissertation, Michigan State University, 1993. Abstract in *Dissertation Abstracts International,* 55, 02A.

Dodd, J. M., Garcia, M., Meccage, C., and Nelson, J. R. "American Indian Student Retention." *NASPA Journal,* 1995, 33, 72–78.

Edgewater, I. L. "Stress and the Navajo University Student." *Journal of American Indian Education,* 1981, 20(3), 25–31.

Falk, D. R., and Aitken, L. P. "Promoting Retention Among American Indian College Students." *Journal of American Indian Education,* 1984, 23(2), 24–31.

Garrod, A., and Larimore, C. *First Person, First Peoples: Native American College Graduates Tell Their Life Stories.* Ithaca, NY: Cornell University Press, 1997.

Heavyrunner, I., and DeCelles, R. "Family Education Model: Meeting the Student Retention Challenge." *Journal of American Indian Education,* 2002, 41(2), 29–37.

Heavyrunner, I., and Morris, J. S. "Traditional Native Culture and Resilience." *Research/Practice,* 1997, 5(1). http://education.umn.edu/carei/Reports/Rpractice/Spring97/traditional.htm.

Heinrich, R. K., Corbine, J. L., and Thomas, K. R. "Counseling Native Americans." *Journal of Counseling and Development,* 1990, 69, 128–133.

Hornett, D. "The Role of Faculty in Cultural Awareness and Retention of American Indian College Students." *Journal of American Indian Education,* 1989, 29(1), 12–18.

Huffman, T. E. "The Experiences, Perception, and Consequences of Campus Racism Among Northern Plains Indians." *Journal of American Indian Education,* 1991, 30(2), 25–34.

Huffman, T. E. "Resistance Theory and the Transculturation Hypothesis as Explanations of College Attrition and Persistence Among Culturally Traditional American Indian Students." *Journal of American Indian Education,* 2001, 40(3), 1–23.

Huffman, T. E., Sill, M. L., and Brokenleg, M. "College Achievement Among Sioux and White South Dakota Students." *Journal of American Indian Education,* 1986, 25(2), 32–38.

Jackson, A. P., and Smith, S. A. "Postsecondary Transitions Among Navajo Students." *Journal of American Indian Education,* 2001, 40(2), 28–47.

Jenkins, M. "Factors Which Influence the Success or Failure of American Indian/Native American College Students." *Research and Teaching in Developmental Education,* 1999, 15(20), 49–52.

Kidwell, C. S. *The Status of Native American Women in Higher Education.* Berkeley: University of California, 1976. (ED 200 364)

Kidwell, C. S. *Motivating American Indians into Graduate Studies* (ERIC Digest). Las Cruces, N.M.: ERIC Clearinghouse on Rural Education and Small Schools, 1986. (ED 286 703)

Kidwell, C. S. *American Indians in Graduate Education.* Washington, D.C.: Council of Graduate Schools in the U.S., 1989. (ED 310 643)

King, P. "Improving Access and Educational Success for Diverse Students: Steady Progress but Enduring Problems." American College Personnel Association, 2001. http://www.myacpa.org. Accessed Dec. 27, 2004.

Kirkness, V. J., and Barnhardt, R. "First Nations and Higher Education: The Four R's—Respect, Relevance, Reciprocity, and Responsibility." *Journal of American Indian Education*, 1991, *30*(3), 1–15.

Kleinfeld, J., Cooper, J., and Kyle, N. "Postsecondary Counselors: A Model for Increasing Native Americans' College Success." *Journal of American Indian Education*, 1987, *27*(1), 9–16.

Kleinfeld, J. S., and Kahout, K. L. "Increasing the College Success of Alaska Natives." *Journal of American Indian Education*, 1974, *13*(3), 27–31.

Laden, B. K., Millem, J. F., and Crowson, R. L. "New Institutional Theory and Student Departure." In J. M. Braxton (ed.), *Reworking the Student Departure Puzzle*. Nashville, Tenn.: Vanderbilt University Press, 2000.

Lin, R., LaCounte, D., and Eder, J. "A Study of Native American Students in a Predominantly White College." *Journal of American Indian Education*, 1988, *27*(3), 8–15.

Locust, C. "Wounding the Spirit: Discrimination and Traditional American Indian Belief Systems." *Harvard Educational Review*, 1988, *58*(3), 315–330.

Loo, C., and Rolison, G. "Alienation of Ethnic Minority Students at a Predominantly White University." *Journal of Higher Education*, 1986, *57*(1), 58–77.

Mayo, J. R., Murguia, E., and Padilla, R. V. "Social Integration and Academic Performance Among Minority University Students." *Journal of College Student Development*, 1995, *36*, 542–552.

Murguia, E., Padilla, R. V., and Pavel, M. "Ethnicity and the Concept of Social Integration in Tinto's Model of Institutional Departure." *Journal of College Student Development*, 1991, *32*, 433–439.

National Center for Education Statistics. *The Condition of Education 2002*. http://nces.ed.gov/pubs2002/2002025.pdf. Accessed Dec. 27, 2004.

Neisler, O. "Access and Retention Strategies in Higher Education: An Introductory Overview." In M. Lang and C. A. Ford (eds.), *Strategies for Retaining Minority Students in Higher Education*. Springfield, Ill.: Thomas, 1992.

Osborne, V., and Cranney, G. A. *Elements of Success in a University Program for Indian Students*. 1985. (ED 257 611) http://www.eric.ed.gov. Accessed Dec. 27, 2004.

Pace, R. C. "Achievement and the Quality of Student Effort." Paper presented at a meeting of the National Commission on Excellence in Education, Washington, D.C., 1982.

Pascarella, E. T. "Racial Differences in Factors Associated with Bachelor's Degree Completion." *Research in Higher Education*, 1985, *23*(4), 351–373.

Pascarella, E. T., and Terenzini, P. T. *How College Affects Students: Findings and Insights from Twenty Years of Research*. San Francisco: Jossey-Bass, 1991.

Patton, W., and Eddington, E. D. "Factors Related to the Persistence of Indian Students at College Level." *Journal of American Indian Education*, 1973, *12*(3), 19–23.

Pavel, D. M. *American Indians and Alaska Natives in Higher Education: Research on Participation and Graduation* (ERIC Digest). Charleston, W.V.: ERIC Clearinghouse on Rural Education and Small Schools, 1992. (ED 348 197)

Pavel, D. M., and Padilla, R. V. "American Indian and Alaska Native Postsecondary Departure: An Example of Assessing a Mainstream Model Using National Longitudinal Data." *Journal of American Indian Education*, 1993, *32*(2), 1–23.

Peregoy, J. J. "Stress and the Sheepskin: An Exploration of the Indian/Native Perspective in College." Doctoral dissertation DAI 52, 04A, Syracuse University, 1990.

Perry, B. "American Indian Victims of Campus Ethnoviolence." *Journal of American Indian Education*, 2002, *41*(1), 35–55.

Reyhner, J., and Dodd, J. "Factors Affecting the Retention of American Indian and Alaska Native Students in Higher Education." Paper presented at the first annual conference of Expanding Minority Opportunities, Tempe, Ariz., Jan. 1995.

Rindone, P. "Achievement Motivation and Academic Achievement of Native American Students." *Journal of American Indian Education*, 1988, 28(1), 1–8.

Scott, W. J. "Attachment to Indian Culture and the 'Different Situation': A Study of American Indian College Students." *Youth and Society*, 1986, 17(4), 381–395.

Shutiva, C. L. *Career and Academic Guidance for American Indian and Alaska Native Youth.* Charleston, W.V.: ERIC Clearinghouse on Rural Education and Small Schools, 2001. (EDORC 013)

Stoecker, J., Pascarella, E. T., and Wolfle, L. M. "Persistence in Higher Education: A Nine-Year Test of a Theoretical Model." *Journal of College Student Development*, 1988, 29, 196–209.

Swail, W. S., and Holmes, D. "Minority Student Persistence: A Model for Colleges and Universities." In S. T. Gregory (ed.), *Academic Achievement of Minority Students: Perspectives, Practices, and Prescriptions.* Latham, Md.: University Press of America, 2000.

Swisher, K. G., and Tippeconnic, J. W., III. "Research to Support Improved Practice in Indian Education." In K. G. Swisher and J. W. Tippeconnic III (eds.), *Next Steps: Research and Practice to Advance Indian Education.* Charleston, W.V.: ERIC Clearinghouse on Rural Education and Small Schools, 1999.

Tate, D. S., and Schwartz, C. L. "Increasing the Retention of American Indian Students in Professional Programs in Higher Education." *Journal of American Indian Education*, 1993, 33(1), 21–31.

Tierney, W. G. "Native Voices in Academe: Strategies for Empowerment." *Change*, 1991, 23(2), 36–45.

Tierney, W. G. "An Anthropological Analysis of Student Participation in College." *Journal of Higher Education*, 1992a, 63, 603–618.

Tierney, W. G. *Official Encouragement, Institutional Discouragement: Minorities in Academe—The Native American Experience.* Norwood, N.J.: Ablex, 1992b.

Tijerina, K., and Biemer, P. "The Dance of Indian Higher Education." *Education Record*, 1988, 68(4), 87–93.

Tinto, V. "Dropout from Higher Education: A Theoretical Synthesis of Recent Research." *Review of Educational Research*, 1975, 45, 89–125.

Tinto, V. "Theory of Student Departure Revisited." In J. Smart (ed.), *Higher Education: Handbook of Theory and Research*, vol. 2. New York: Agathon Press, 1986.

Turner, S. "Federal Financial Aid: How Well Does It Work?" In J. C. Smart (ed.), *Higher Education: Handbook of Theory and Research*, vol. 6. New York: Agathon Press, 2001.

United States Office of Education. "Higher Education of Southwestern Indians with Reference to Success and Failure." Journal of American Indian Education, 1965, 4(2), 5–13.

Whitehorse, D. M. "Cultural Identification and Institutional Character: Retention Factors for American Indian Students in Higher Education." Doctoral dissertation AAG9307281, Northern Arizona University, 1992.

Wright, B. "Programming Success: Special Student Services and the American Indian College Student." *Journal of American Indian Education*, 1985, 24(1), 1–7.

Wright, B. "American Indian Studies Programs: Surviving the '80s, Thriving in the '90s." *Journal of American Indian Education*, 1990, 30(1), 17–24.

Wright, B. "The Untameable Savage Spirit: American Indians in Colonial Colleges." *Review of Higher Education*, 1991, 14(4), 429–452.

Wright, D. J. "Minority Students: Developmental Beginnings." In D. J. Wright (ed.), *Responding to the Needs of Today's Minority Students.* New Directions for Student Services, no. 38. San Francisco: Jossey-Bass, 1987.

DR. JAMES A. LARIMORE (COMANCHE) is dean of the college at Dartmouth College.

DR. GEORGE S. MCCLELLAN is vice president for student development at Dickinson State University.

3

This chapter shares the experiences of some Native American students in mainstream education and provides recommendations for student affairs professionals working with Native American students.

This Is Who I Am: Experiences of Native American Students

Shelly C. Lowe (Navajo)

The experiences of Native American students in higher education are vast and varied, as are the tribal cultures, traditions, languages, and beliefs of the 562 Indian nations in the United States. To say that all Native American students have the same experience in higher education would be naive. This chapter will give some insight into the experiences of Native American students in higher education, but it is not a story about what to expect from all Native American students. It is merely an introduction, a starting place on a path that each student affairs professional must explore individually when working with Native American students.

The chapter will begin by providing information about Native American student enrollment, persistence, and graduation. It will then present stories of Native American students in higher education. Readers should note that the literature on Native American student experiences in higher education is very sparse, much of it in popular media sources such as regional newspaper and magazine articles. These accounts, along with my own experiences as a student and student affairs professional, will serve as resources for this discussion. The chapter will end with recommendations for student affairs professionals working with Native American students.

Current Participation of Native Americans in Higher Education

The number of Native American students enrolled in higher education began to increase sharply in the late 1960s and early 1970s, spurred by the growing availability of scholarships and funding and the emergence of tribally

NEW DIRECTIONS FOR STUDENT SERVICES, no. 109, Spring 2005 © Wiley Periodicals, Inc.

controlled colleges and universities (Szasz, 1999). The past two decades, however, have seen smaller gains in Native American enrollments. Of the approximately 145,000 Native American students enrolled, roughly 134,000 are in undergraduate study, 10,000 in graduate study, and 1,000 in professional degree programs. Although the number of Native American students enrolled in higher education increased more than 90 percent between 1976 and 1999, the growth in Native American enrollment as a percentage of total enrollment has been more modest (National Center for Educational Statistics, 2001a).

Even though progress has been made in aggregate Native American enrollment over the past twenty years, little has changed with respect to the types of institutions at which Native American students are enrolled. Data show that Native Americans continue to be underrepresented both in the more prestigious private and four-year sectors of higher education and overrepresented in the less prestigious public and two-year sectors. Native Americans are also noticeably underrepresented among college degree recipients (National Center for Education Statistics, 2001b), and this underrepresentation occurs at all degree levels (Morgan, 1999).

Native American Student Experience in College

Will you succeed, or will you leave? New Native American college students are confronted with the pressure of that question even before their first day on campus. The experiences of other students who are Native American makes it hard not to be familiar with the trends in Native American college student persistence and graduation. One young Navajo woman preparing to enter her freshman year reflected this awareness when she shared that she is fully aware eyes will be on her and watching to see how she does and whether or not she succeeds (Duarte, 2000).

One Student's Story. The following is a story of one young Native American woman's experience in higher education. Raised on an Indian reservation where she attended public school from kindergarten through high school, the young woman was accepted at all the state's universities as an honor student and provided with a merit-based tuition waiver at the university she chose to attend. She was also awarded a prestigious college scholarship, covering the cost of attendance for four years at one of the state's public universities (including room and board) and providing funds for two study trips abroad. Everything for college was set; all she had to do was go.

This student had some prior experience on a college campus. Her mother had attended college during the summers when she was younger, and she and her brother lived on campus with her mother. She also had attended summer programs on a college campus. When her brother went to college, she visited him often, but he attended only one year before dropping out. The young woman had not, however, been on the campus of the college she had chosen to attend; nor did she have any familiarity with the city in which the college was located. In fact, the college was roughly a six-hour drive away from her home. Still, she was excited about going to school. Her financial needs were met. She was going to live in the dorm her first year; and she had already spoken by telephone to people in the scholarship office, the honors program, and academic programs, as well current students on campus. They were ready for her arrival, and she was ready to go.

Some of this young woman's high school friends were freshmen on campus. She lived in a campus residence hall with a roommate, and she participated in numerous activities with her honors and scholarship peers. She was assigned a faculty mentor in her area of study, and numerous people were available within the university to offer assistance. But as the semester wore on, she found herself skipping classes more frequently and driving the six hours home more and more often. By the second semester of her first year, she was going home every other weekend, and she barely completed the minimum number of units necessary to maintain satisfactory progress in her first semester. This student returned for the second semester and completed the first year, but she was on probation with her scholarship and did not return the following fall. Despite all her preparations and planning, the young woman's experience at college was not a good one. She was unable to succeed as everyone had hoped, planned, and expected.

This student was not a first-generation college student. A number of people on campus were there to help and guide her. She had the necessary academic ability and financial resources to help assure her success at college. Why did she not succeed? What specific factors caused this student to have such a difficult time adjusting to a large public university? These questions, unfortunately, do not always have clear answers. We can speculate about why this student did not do as well as she could have, but the reality is that neither the student nor the individuals interested in learning what happened may ever be able to pinpoint the reasons. The only way to try to figure out this puzzle is to listen to what this student and others like her have to say and then assess the services and programs intended to help these students.

I have intimate knowledge of this student's story, because that student was me. Although I did return in the spring of my second year, on my return I began to realize that I was trying to be what others were anticipating that I be—a model or typical college student. The model, however, was not applicable. I had to recognize my own identity and strength as a Native American college student. I had to tell people, "This is who I am" so that they could understand where I was coming from and where I intended to go.

Students' Stories. The work of Garrod and Larimore (1997), a collection of stories by Native American graduates of Dartmouth College, stands out as one of the richer contributions to the literature. Each story is unique and compelling in its own right, and each presents a picture of a single Native American student's college experience. Collectively, however, the students' stories offer compelling insights.

Many of these stories address the difficulty of transitioning into college life, depression and loneliness, a desire to return home coupled with the desire to be successful in order to go home with a degree, the people and places that made a difference both on campus and at home, inner strength, and the desire to succeed. These stories tell not only of the college experience but of the background of each student, and from these stories the reader is able to recognize that not all Native American students are alike. The students in these stories come from similar yet extremely different backgrounds. Some are very rooted in their cultures, and some know very little. Some grew up on the reservation, some in urban areas. Some have dealt with racism, alcoholism, poverty, and broken families; others have not. What is similar with each of these stories is that, for their own reasons, each person succeeded and knew what factors led to that success.

In another account (Romero, 2002), a first-time Native American freshman at Princeton University, shares the story of her experience in higher education. Like the student from the earlier story, college turned out not to be what this young woman had expected. Princeton was like nothing she knew. Everything was different from what she grew up with: the land, the weather, the buildings, the people. She didn't feel like she fit into the existing social structure. She was miserable and depressed. She cried and longed to go home, but going home was not a matter of simply getting in the car and driving a few hours or more. Home was two thousand miles from campus. She missed her family and her culture; she missed everything that mattered to her. If not for the reassuring words of her grandfather, two caring cafeteria workers who would ask her about her day and how she was doing, and a faculty member who helped her draw on her cultural strengths in her writing, she would not have been able to stay.

Although she persisted and graduated, her words tell us how difficult life at the university was for her: "Princeton has beaten me. Princeton has made me cry. Princeton has made me feel alone. Princeton has hurt my deepest feelings. All those precepts I felt uncomfortable participating in because I was the only indigenous voice, for that time someone told me 'You live in an Indian box,' and another said, 'There are over 30 Native kids here, why are you complaining?' Princeton has tested my fortitude" (Romero, p. 2).

This student came to Princeton not knowing the social norms of the institution and not feeling that she was an important part of the institution, though she knew she belonged there. She was there for a reason, whether anyone else at Princeton knew this or not. She was there to get an education for herself, her family, and her community. In order to do this, she had to fight stereotypes in her classes and listen to classmates voice their negative ideas and ignorance about Native American cultures. She had to fight to be recognized, but she also had to fight to find the strength to demand recognition. She had to find a way to be comfortable away from home, and she had to believe in her determination to stay until she graduated.

Recommendations

I hope the stories in this chapter have provided some insights into the experiences of Native American students in higher education. Just as these stories vary based on individual and institutional circumstances, so too must the approaches that student affairs professionals use with them. The goal is to help assure that the experiences of Native American students in higher education support those students' success.

The following are recommendations for student affairs professionals to help assure positive experiences for Native American students on their campuses.

• *Work with Native American students prior to their arrival on campus.* If your office is providing a service to them, mail information and instructions ahead of time and periodically check for problems the student may be having or items that the student has not completed. Make it a point to locate and bring Native American students into your office or area as soon as possible after they arrive on campus to complete any necessary paperwork or tasks.

• *Orient the student to the university, both as a campus and as a system.* Realize that many Native American students are not familiar with how a university is organized. At the beginning new students must often work with a number of offices including the registrar, bursar, financial aid, housing, bookstore, and on-campus meal program, to name a few. It is not always clear to students who are Native American how or why programs do or do not work with one another.

• *Orient the student to the local area and to living in the area.* Many Native American students are not familiar with the city in which the campus is located.

• *Help the students feel they are a part of the university family.* For many, this is the first time they have been outside of their tribal communities or away from their families. They may feel different, visible, and misunderstood because they don't fit into the existing social system, have no experience with it, or don't accept it. They may feel that they must constantly explain who they are, where they come from, and why they are here.

• *Students must have some place where they feel they belong.* Programs and services with Native American faculty and staff often become this place because of the Native American presence, but other programs need to find ways to bring that presence into their own programs.

• *Find out what local services are available to Native Americans.* Some communities have Indian centers or programs that can assist Native Americans with such things as utility payments, child care, and transportation. Indian Health Service clinics or hospitals can also provide much-needed assistance for Native American students and their families who are away from home. Find out which, if any, of these services are available in your area and be knowledgeable about where they are located and how to access them.

• *Provide help and be proactive about it.* Realize that not all students who are Native American know how to ask for help, know where to go for help, or feel comfortable asking for help. Be proactive in working with these students. If you see or foresee a problem, don't wait for the student to come to you. Be proactive in contacting that student in order to get things solved. Ask the student if there is anything else he or she needs to do and be able to point the student in the right direction to get it done.

• *Never generalize; treat each student as a unique person.* Understand that not all Native American students have the same backgrounds, experiences, cultural traditions, or knowledge of higher education. The worst thing to do is to stereotype Native American students or assume they all have the same problems. Instead, be sure to ask questions that allow you to get insight into that individual student's situation without seeming overly forward. Give suggestions and direction based on the individual situation. Take time to hear and learn each student's story in order to work with that student and other Native American students as well as for your own growth. The more you learn about different Native American student experiences, the more tools you will have to work with in student affairs.

• *Orient yourself to Native models or ways of thinking.* Do not rely solely on established development models; they may not be applicable to students who are Native American. Tribes and Native American cultures have their own development models and theories of education. Try to learn some of these and take them into consideration when working with Native American students. Also, be careful not to develop a generic all-purpose "Indian" model; it may not be appropriate for use with students of different tribal nations.

• *Foster and support the student's Native identity.* Some students have very strong Native American identities as they enter college. Others come far less connected to that aspect of their identities. In either case, the experience of Native American students in higher education will shape and be shaped by their Native American identity.

• *Focus on the importance of schoolwork and classes.* Understand that in many cases, students who are Native American do not come to college to "find themselves" or to learn to be adults. Native American students come to college to learn, but college is school and in many cases nothing more. They come to college to get an academic degree, and they are on campus for the sole purpose of going to class and getting their schoolwork done. It is important to recognize that school needs to be addressed first and foremost for a lot of these students, as opposed to the social aspect of college.

• *Find ways to identify and nurture Native American students' own strengths.* Students who are Native American most likely have all the inner strength they need to succeed. It has been a part of their lives since birth, formed and nurtured throughout their lives. It is the connection and belief in their families, traditions, language, and culture. It is their tie to their home and to the people and places at home. This is the strength they will draw on to succeed. Finding ways to help these students draw on this strength could make a powerful difference. It may be helpful for students to reflect on who they are, where they come from, and why they are here.

• *Perceive and treat each Native student as able to succeed.* Every Native student on a college campus is already a success. These students have already overcome obstacles to get where they are today. Native students in college not only graduated high school but were also accepted into college. Not every student is accepted, but these students were. They all have the necessary skills to succeed. Some may just need assistance in recognizing those skills.

• *Conduct more research.* This recommendation is plain and simple: there needs to be more research regarding the experiences of Native American students in higher education. Student affairs professionals, graduate students, graduate preparation programs, researchers, and institutions need to make a priority of engaging in research toward that end.

It is well past time to combat approaches to education research that marginalize Native American students. Footnotes indicating that findings on Native Americans are not statistically significant and so are omitted from the research are too often the only reference to Native Americans in much of the literature in higher education. Such footnotes are no longer acceptable as results. The Native student population may not be large, depending on where you look for it, but it is important and worthy of study.

Qualitative research takes time, but already too much time has gone by without an adequate volume of research on the experiences of Native American students. Native students need to be asked about their experiences and given the opportunity to tell their story.

Conclusion

It is very important to remember that the success of even one Native student brings success to a larger group. Native Americans take great pride in the success and achievement of their students, who are being looked on as leaders for the future. These students are in a very unique position because their success or failure will affect their family, tribes, and communities.

Although Native American students may interact with many professionals on campus, sometimes the support and assistance of just one person can make the difference. This person becomes a friend, mentor, and adviser. This person is someone to whom the student can come whenever he or she needs help. This person listens, understands, and relates to the student. Being this one person in a Native student's college career is one of the most positive rewards one can have in student affairs. We should all strive to be rewarded in this way.

References

Duarte, C. "UA's Indian Students: The Few Among Many." *Arizona Daily Star*, Aug. 24, 2000, p. C15.

Garrod, A., and Larimore, C. *First Person, First Peoples: Native American College Graduates Tell Their Life Stories.* Ithaca, N.Y.: Cornell University Press, 1997.

Morgan, F. B. *Degrees and Other Awards Conferred by Title IV Eligible, Degree-Granting Institutions: 1996–1997* (NCES 2000–174, table A). Washington, D.C.: National Center for Education Statistics, U.S. Department of Education, 1999. http://nces.ed.gov/pubsearch/pubsinfo.asp?pubid=2000166a.

National Center for Education Statistics. *Digest of Educational Statistics, 2001.* Washington, D.C.: U.S. Department of Education, 2001a. http://nces.ed.gov/pubs2002/digest2001/tables/dt208.asp.

National Center for Education Statistics. *Digest of Educational Statistics, 2001.* Washington, D.C.: U.S. Department of Education, 2001b. http://nces.ed.gov/pubs2002/digest2001/tables/dt207.asp.

Romero, A. "Leaving the Comforts of Home to Help Preserve the Cochiti Legacy." *Daily Princetonian News,* Dec. 11, 2002. http://www.dailyprincetonian.com/archives/2002/12/11/page3/#6642. Accessed Jan. 31, 2003.

Szasz, M. C. *Education and the American Indian: The Road to Self-Determination Since 1928.* (3rd ed.) Albuquerque: University of New Mexico Press, 1999.

SHELLY C. LOWE (NAVAJO) *is a doctoral candidate in higher education at the University of Arizona.*

The author offers insights into perceptions and expectations that tribal leaders and Native American parents have of higher education.

Perspectives of American Indian Nation Parents and Leaders

Raymond D. Austin (Navajo)

The idea that American Indians and Alaska Natives should be educated in the Western institutions of higher learning so that they can participate in the Western ways of life is older than the United States. Thousands of pages of official policies, laws, court decisions, studies, and reports attest that educating American Indians in Western ways has always been a Euro-American obsession. Education for American Indians by Euro-Americans, however, has produced few laudable achievements, because its proponents did not bother to consult with American Indian parents, American Indian communities, and American Indian leaders about their children's education.

American Indians have been studying at the colleges and universities in this country for 350 years now, yet the key people at these institutions—administrators, student services staff, and faculty–can claim no more than exiguous knowledge about the American Indian students on their campuses. If institutions of higher education want to improve their American Indian retention and graduation rates, they must include American Indian views and expectations in their planning. To date, however, these institutions have expressed little interest in knowing the views of tribal leaders and the parents of their American Indian students. Although not presuming to represent the view of all leaders or all parents, this chapter seeks to offer insights into perceptions and expectations that tribal leaders and parents have of higher education. The chapter discusses five major areas: tribal legal status, funding for American Indian college students, support for American Indian students, cooperative relationships between universities and American Indian nations, and respect for American Indian cultures and languages.

NEW DIRECTIONS FOR STUDENT SERVICES, no. 109, Spring 2005 © Wiley Periodicals, Inc.

Tribal Legal Status

Most Americans know of the two sovereigns—federal and state—operating in the United States, but most are not aware that American Indian nations form a third sovereign. The United States Constitution and nearly 175 years of United States Supreme Court decisions have recognized the American Indian tribes as limited-sovereign nations possessing inherent powers of self-government, which necessarily includes the power to govern their internal relations and regulate their territories. The American Indian nations interact with each other, the U.S. government, and the state governments on a government-to-government basis. This relationship underlies the many intergovernmental agreements that the officials of these sovereigns have signed over the years.

It is easy for colleges and universities to simply dismiss students who are American Indian as just another minority group clamoring for special attention, but things are not that simple. Unlike other minority groups, American Indians have "maintained a special relationship to American society and its governing bodies" since the early days of the republic (Woodcock and Alawiye, 2001, p. 810). Although the American public has strong sentiments about equality and equal opportunity, federal policies, laws, and court decisions have created separate standards for American Indians pursuant to the unique federal-tribal relationship (called trust relationship)—a political relationship deeply embedded in the nation's historical dealings with its original inhabitants. Awareness of this special relationship would help key college and university officials better understand their American Indian students, the students' tribes, and the responsibilities the universities have assumed by admitting American Indian students.

Support for American Indian Students

American Indian students are an invisible minority on most campuses; and institutional apathy for their well-being has fostered misunderstanding, miscommunication, stereotyping, campus racism, and marginalization of American Indian students. University information that shows American Indian student enrollment counts and graduation and dropout rates can say a lot about an institution's level of commitment to its American Indian students, American Indian programs, and overall campus diversity. These statistics can influence the parents of potential American Indian college students, particularly those living on reservations, when selecting a university. A university that works hard at recruiting and retaining students who are American Indian usually enjoys a large American Indian enrollment and favorable retention and graduation rates for those students. American Indian parents will gladly send their children to a university that values its American Indian students as part of the university community.

Parental Expectations. American Indian parents (like potential American Indian college students) usually favor a university with a large American Indian enrollment and positive retention and graduation rates as the university to attend. A large American Indian enrollment allows the students to develop a support system to help each other. The university usually has programs that give special attention to the needs of students who are American Indian such as a residence wing for freshman and sophomore American Indian students, precollege orientation for American Indian students, socials to connect American Indian students with each other, group registration for American Indian students, and mentors and tutors who are American Indian. Moreover, universities with large American Indian student enrollments normally have American Indian faculty and administrators, American Indian studies programs, majors and minors in American Indian programs, working relationships with American Indian nations and tribal communities, and faculty knowledgeable about American Indian issues. These factors also carry tremendous weight when American Indian parents and students choose a university.

American Indian parents do not want their children to start college without assistance, nor do they want their children overwhelmed with college adjustment problems. American Indian students, particularly those from reservations, can find the freshman year of college daunting. Adjustment problems and culture shock can send even the most academically qualified Indian student packing a month into the semester. Universities can relieve the anxiety by making graduate and upper-division students who are American Indians available to help new American Indian students maneuver the college maze. Programs and functions that connect American Indian students to each other and to American Indian faculty and administrators can also provide much-needed support.

American Indian parents want their children to establish good relationships with their professors. A professor knows when a student is having problems and should take the initiative to help that student. A professor should recommend the American Indian student to student services if he or she is unable to help. A caring professor can prevent the American Indian student from acting on the "I should just go home" feeling. Student services can also practice preventive measures by tracking at-risk Indian students throughout the school year and quickly helping when the need arises.

Tribal Expectations. Leaders of American Indian tribes have unique expectations when it comes to higher education for their students. They want American Indian students to soak up Western knowledge, place that knowledge within the context of their cultures and languages, and return home to better their communities. Tribal expectations cannot be fulfilled unless American Indian students remain in college. Tribes have therefore given gifts to universities with instructions to do everything possible to retain their students and improve the American Indian graduation rate. These gifts should be used to provide the students who meet the university's definition of *American Indian* with academic tutoring, counseling, mentoring, emergency grants or loans, and other services to improve the retention rate of American Indian students.

University and American Indian Nation Partnerships

There are many areas in which American Indian nations and institutions of higher education cooperate (or should cooperate) to address Indian country problems and needs. Universities are repositories of knowledge and expertise, so American Indian nations desire mutually beneficial relationships with them. The tribes know that the institutions they can turn to for help maintain a core group of American Indian students; have American Indian faculty or faculty knowledgeable about Indian issues; and offer American Indian studies programs, American Indian law programs, American Indian education programs, or other programs that train students for work with American Indian communities and American Indian nation governments.

Research Partnerships. Occasionally, tribal officials encounter problems and issues that require study by outside experts. The tribes' unique sovereign status can generate eclectic issues that require specialized knowledge and skill. American Indian tribes may also encounter social, health, or economic problems that require specialized inquiry within the tribe's cultural context; and a tribe-university effort might be necessary. The American Indian diabetes epidemic is one such example. These kinds of problems and issues require university and tribe agreements that contain guidelines for the research or study and the methods of reporting findings and recommendations to tribal officials. Unique issues arise in the fields of American Indian education, American Indian health, and reservation economics; and these areas produce prime opportunities for tribe and university partnerships.

Tribes Need Graduates. Very few American Indians have earned bachelor's degrees. Only 9.3 percent of the American Indian population in the United States, ages twenty-five and older, had earned undergraduate degrees by 1995 compared to 20.3 percent of the non-Indian population (Dingman, Mroczka, and Brady, 1995). Even fewer American Indians hold graduate and professional degrees. Because tribes drastically need college-educated talent, universities should improve on the number of American Indians receiving degrees in the fields of law, medicine, business, American Indian language and culture preservation, agriculture, education, health, engineering, administration, and management. Some universities have accepted the challenge to graduate more American Indians in these fields, and we applaud them. More colleges and universities should join the effort. American Indian college graduates are needed to work with tribal communities, schools that educate American Indian children, health care providers, tribe-owned businesses, and American Indian nation governments. Tribal leadership also needs American Indians with graduate and professional degrees to do research and help develop Indian policy.

Training Teachers and Administrators. The field of American Indian education is chronically short of American Indian teachers, principals, and superintendents. American Indians with degrees in education are needed to move American Indian education forward. Those graduates have knowledge of American Indian cultures and languages that make them ideally suited for working with schools that educate American Indian children, with American Indian pupils and their parents, and with the local American Indian communities. The teachers and administrators that American Indian education needs most are those capable of using American Indian cultures and traditional teaching methods to motivate and educate American Indian children. We know that local control of schools promotes community and parent involvement in education. The school becomes the hub of community life on a reservation. Community-oriented schools have even helped boost economic development opportunities in American Indian communities (Szasz, 1999). American Indian teachers and administrators who know their cultures and apply them in the schools and tribal communities are the key to local control of schools and American Indian education shedding its assimilationist practices.

University officials who have experience with American Indian issues know that educators who are American Indian have positively influenced reservation schools and empowered tribal communities, so they have accepted the challenge to graduate more teachers and administrators who are American Indian. For example, some colleges and universities have joined with the Navajo Nation to develop teacher-training programs that accommodate Navajo students, Navajo culture, and the rural Navajo lifestyle. Schools serving Navajo children on the Navajo Nation need skilled Navajo teachers who can integrate Navajo culture, history, and language into the curriculum. When it comes to teaching American Indian children, knowing only Western teaching methods is not enough. The differences between American Indian cultures and American mainstream culture produce challenges that require application of both Western and traditional American Indian teaching methods.

Distance Education. Some colleges and universities are helping American Indian education by instructing their college students using distance education programs. Students enrolled in distance education programs work in their communities during the day and attend college classes using either the Internet or other telecommunications technology in the evening. University distance education has great potential for American Indians who reside on rural reservations (Sanchez, Stuckey, and Morris, 1998). American Indians, like other Americans, value education; but family and cultural obligations, financial hardships, and employment often make attending college far from home difficult. The key to successful distance education for American Indians is cultural sensitivity: the college must understand that the students are "part of the cultural community," and it must be "sensitive to the parameters of that community, recognizing that 'distance' can be both cultural and geographic, and that effective learning requires the reduction of both" (p. 7).

Tribal Colleges. Tribal colleges have worked miracles in American Indian higher education: "Tribal colleges have proven their ability to enroll students who were not served by higher education, to graduate students who have dropped out of other institutions, and to sponsor successful community development projects" (Pavel, 1999, p. 249). Tribal colleges enroll more than thirty thousand students (Boyer, 2002). If we want to move Indian higher education to the next level and improve on the American Indian matriculation and graduation rates, we have to include tribal colleges in the plan.

While operating under the most trying circumstances, the tribal colleges have been able to retain their students and help raise the college matriculation rate of American Indians. They have significant knowledge of strategies for retaining American Indian students that mainstream colleges and universities could use (Pavel, 1992). Tribal colleges are also committed to preserving and revitalizing American Indian cultures and languages, which could lead to mutually beneficial partnerships with mainstream institutions. Mainstream colleges and universities would be wise to seek out mutually beneficial partnerships with tribal colleges.

Tribal colleges perform a critical role in the ongoing mission to graduate more teachers, administrators, and other professionals who are American Indians. Some tribal colleges have joined with four-year institutions by developing and offering programs that allow American Indian students to complete their first two years of study at the tribal college and then transfer to the university to complete the remaining major requirements (Pavel, Inglebret, and Banks, 2001). Tribal colleges can work with mainstream institutions to make distance education programs available to American Indian students who live in remote areas. The cooperation and goodwill between tribal colleges and mainstream universities should expand to more programs, including nursing, preservation of language and culture, natural resources, economic development, and fields in which tribes and tribal communities need college-educated American Indian professionals.

Respect American Indian Cultures and Languages

American Indians have 350 years of experience with Western higher education in the United States. For the majority of this time, Western higher education has relegated Indian cultures to the category of myth while anointing Western perspectives with the status of truth. This method of education has produced American Indian college graduates who are at odds with their own American Indian communities. The conflicted graduate cannot function effectively in either mainstream society or the American Indian society. American Indian college graduates indoctrinated with

Western perspectives have caused turmoil within their tribes by favoring Western values, exploitation, and economics over their own cultures, values, and beliefs. Consequently, corporations have snatched up tribal natural resources for pennies and left tribes with ravaged lands, destroyed sacred sites, and polluted air and water. American Indian college graduates have a duty to use their Western-acquired technical skills and knowledge within the American Indian context when working with tribal governments and communities.

American Indians are revitalizing their cultures and languages all across America. There must be respect for American Indian cultures, languages, land, and all our relatives in the natural world. Institutions of higher education can help by acknowledging that American Indian cultures and languages are as essential to human survival as any other subject. Colleges and universities should demonstrate that American Indians matter by offering courses on American Indian history, cultures, and languages; encouraging internships with tribal governments and communities; inviting American Indian leaders and elders as speakers; and promoting faculty and student exchange programs with tribal colleges.

Conclusion and Recommendations

Colleges and universities can prevent and eliminate existing misconceptions and miscommunications by sponsoring American Indian cultural awareness programs at which faculty, administrators, and non-Native students can exchange information and concerns with tribal leaders, American Indian parents, and American Indian students. Tribal leaders and parents should be invited to roundtable discussions to give their views on matters that affect American Indian students, including recruitment, retention, high school preparation, summer precollege programs, adequate financial aid, student support programs, integration of tribal culture into courses, growth in the number of American Indian faculty and administrators, and the elimination of racism and prejudice. Every avenue that is conducive to the academic and social success of American Indian students in college should be explored. The tribal officials, American Indian parents, and tribal communities must likewise do their part by supporting and encouraging their students to take advantage of higher education and graduate. Challenges abound in American Indian higher education, but through communication and cooperation tribes and universities can produce American Indian college graduates who are in tune with tribal societies.

References

Boyer, P. "Defying the Odds." *Tribal College Journal,* 2002, *14*(2), 12–19.
Dingman, S. M., Mroczka, M. A., and Brady, J. V. "Predicting Academic Success for American Indian Students." *Journal of American Indian Education,* 1995, *34*(2), 10–17.

Pavel, D. M. *American Indians and Alaska Natives in Higher Education: Research on Participation and Graduation.* ERIC Digest. Charleston, W.Va.: ERIC Clearinghouse on Rural Education and Small Schools, 1992. (ED 348 197)

Pavel, D. M. "American Indians and Alaska Natives in Higher Education: Promoting Access and Achievement." In K. G. Swisher and J. W. Tippeconnic III (eds.), *Next Steps: Research and Practice to Advance Indian Education.* Charleston, W.Va.: ERIC Clearinghouse on Rural Education and Small Schools, 1999.

Pavel, D. M., Inglebret, E., and Banks, S. R. "Tribal Colleges and Universities in an Era of Dynamic Development." *Peabody Journal of Education,* 2001, 76(1), 50–72.

Sanchez, J., Stuckey, M. E., and Morris, R. "Distance Learning in Indian Country: Becoming the Spider on the Web." *Journal of American Indian Education,* 1998, 37(3), 1–17.

Szasz, M. C. *Education and the American Indian: The Road to Self-Determination Since 1928.* (3rd ed.) Albuquerque: University of New Mexico Press, 1999.

Woodcock, D. B., and Alawiye, O. "The Antecedents of Failure and Emerging Hope: American Indians and Public Higher Education." *Education,* 2001, 121(4), 810–820.

RAYMOND D. AUSTIN, J.D. (NAVAJO) is a doctoral student in American Indian Studies at the University of Arizona. He served sixteen years on the Navajo Nation Supreme Court.

*What is the role of Native American faculty and staff in
majority institutions with relation to Native American
students? This chapter provides recommendations for
student affairs professionals and further research.*

Voices from Within: Native American Faculty and Staff on Campus

Mary Jo Tippeconnic Fox (Comanche)

Faculty and staff in higher education play a vital role in student development and student learning (Pascarella and Terenzini, 1991), and faculty and
staff from underrepresented groups can play a particularly important role
in the development and learning of students from those groups in majority
institutions (Wilson, 1998). What impact do Native American faculties have
on the experiences of Native American students in such institutions? How
can having Native Americans as faculty and staff in positions within majority institutions assist non-Native student affairs professionals in serving
Native American students? How do the experiences of Native American faculty and staff at majority institutions affect their ability to provide support
for Native American students either directly or in partnership with non-
Native allies? These are important questions given the critical human
resource needs in Indian country, the growing number of Native American
students entering majority institutions of higher education, and the far more
modest increase in the number of Native American faculty and staff at such
institutions. Despite their importance, these questions have been the subject of little research or discussion in higher education. This chapter seeks
to address these critically important questions. In doing so, it is intended to
serve as the beginning of a conversation about Native American faculty and
staff in mainstream institutions of higher education, the role they can play
in supporting Native American students, and the ways in which they can
collaborate with non-Native faculty and staff in supporting those students.
It is a conversation that needs to occur among students, parents, faculty,
administrators, staff, and alumni who are serious about supporting Native
American students.

The chapter begins with a review of the literature on the impact of faculty and staff on the higher education experiences of Native American students. A description of the structural representation and stratification of Native Americans among faculty and staff in higher education follows, and the chapter then addresses the experiences of those faculty and staff members. Next, the chapter discusses the implications of the relative scarcity of Native American faculty and staff with respect to the work of non-Native colleagues in supporting the success of Native American students. After presenting personal reflections, the chapter concludes with recommendations for practice and future research.

Role of Faculty and Staff in Native American Student Success

A number of scholars have addressed the impact of faculty and staff on success for Native American students in mainstream higher education (Terenzini, Pascarella, and Blimling, 1996; Swisher, Hoisch, and Pavel, 1991; Brown and Kurpius Robinson, 1997). They report that interaction with faculty and staff has a positive effect on the academic success and persistence of Native American students. Attaining social integration with faculty can be crucial to the educational persistence of Native American students according to Pavel and Padilla (1993).

How is this positive impact realized? Tierney (1995) states that students, especially Native American students, need to form a relationship with at least one instructor per term by attending office hours. Jackson, Smith, and Hill (2003) found that successful Native American college students identified a perception of warmth from faculty and staff as one of the factors in their persistence. It made Native American students feel someone cared about them. One student who participated in the study said, "I think once I realized that professors are so willing to help you, you're much more willing to go in and say, 'I need help with this'" (p. 554). Hornett (1989, p. 13) states that professors can create an appropriate, positive, academic environment in which to learn: "It isn't required that the faculty be Indian, they only need to be student oriented, caring individuals who are open to innovative ideas that may change the normal routine of their teaching styles and classroom presentations." According to Hornett, institutions of higher education wishing to promote retention of Native American students must ensure that faculty and staff are culturally aware and prepared to employ different methods than they use with white students.

Other scholars have specifically addressed the benefits to Native American students of having access to Native American faculty and staff on campus. Native American students have concerns about the lack of cultural knowledge about Native Americans that non-Native faculty and staff in mainstream higher education have (Tierney, 1992), and Native American students' feelings of isolation may be attributed in part to the perception that some non-Native faculty and staff are hostile (Lin, LaCounte, and Eder, 1988). Although acknowledging that students benefit from a good relationship with any teacher, Swisher and Tippeconnic (1999) emphasize that if the teacher happens to be Native American and a good teacher, the relationship is often enhanced. Though they were referring specifically to K–12 teachers, we might extend the thought to higher education as well. Stein (2003, p. 49) on faculty in tribal colleges states, "Indigenous instructors can, in addition to being good teachers, be wonderful role models for the local indigenous students." In her study of Native American completers in a tribal college, Ness (2002) also found the importance of hiring qualified Native American faculty and staff to promote a welcoming atmosphere and provide role models for Native American students. Bergstrom, Cleary, and Peacock (2003, p. 171) state, "Native teachers have an easier time figuring out what is needed than teachers who are culturally different from the students they teach. What Native teachers have over non-Native teachers is experience with many of the same issues Native youth now confront on a daily basis." Tippeconnic and McKinney (2003) state that one strategy for recruiting and retaining Native American students is to recruit, retain, and promote more Native American faculty because they serve as role models and work with Native American students to ensure academic success. Actively working to recruit, retain, and promote Native American faculty and staff also serves as an indication of an institution's commitment to diversity (Falk and Aitken, 1984).

Structural Representation and Stratification

Less than one half of one percent of all staff in higher education are Native American, and the same can be said of professional staff (National Center for Education Statistics, 2001a). Given the variances in definitions for the field, it is not surprising that no reliable statistics are available regarding the number of Native American student affairs professionals.

Roughly three-quarters of one percent of all faculty in higher education are Native American. Although 7.5 percent of all Native Americans have achieved the rank of full professor, Native Americans make up only 0.2 percent of all full professors in higher education (National Center for Education Statistics, 2001b).

In addition, very few Native Americans are among the ranks of senior administrators in higher education. Harvey (2002) reports a Native American president at only twenty-one institutions, of which fourteen were tribally controlled institutions.

Experiences of Native American Faculty and Staff

Although no literature is available regarding the experiences of Native American staff in higher education, a modest amount is available on the experiences of Native American faculty. Given their scarcity on campuses and the fact that they must represent Native Americans in teaching, service, and research, Native American faculty can become overburdened through institutional expectations to develop new courses with Native American content, represent all Native Americans in informal and formal interactions, and have expertise related to the Native American experience in all areas (Kidwell, 1990). Stein (1996, p. 394) states: "American Indian faculty, junior or senior, find they are expected by students, colleagues, and administrators to serve as mentors, advisors, and role models to all American Indian students, and even all other minority students on campus." This can be a heavy burden for Native American faculty, one that their non-Native colleagues do not always share. Though advising and mentoring Native American students can be very rewarding for Native American faculty and staff, it can be time-consuming, especially when many non-Native professionals and administrators within the institutions refer Native American students to Native faculty and staff instead of working with them themselves. The additional burden of institutional (or self-imposed) expectations becomes even more problematic for junior Native American faculty working toward tenure (Cross, 1991). Cook-Lynn (1996) addresses herself specifically to the challenges of Native American women in academia, which include supporting or denying their historical legacies. Stein (1996) found many Native American faculty members frustrated to the point that they intended to move on to other careers. These faculty members felt their colleagues perceived them as having been hired because they were Native Americans. The Native American faculty were also frustrated by the marginalization of their research and by the sense that they had to work harder than their colleagues in order to earn respect as scholars.

In a related article, Verdugo (1995) argued that if institutions of higher education want to use Hispanic faculty as role models, the institution must first address ideological and structural factors that relegate them to second-class status. Without addressing this, institutions that use Hispanic faculty as role models will send a negative image to students. One can make a similar argument with respect to Native American faculty.

Implications for Non-Native Faculty and Staff

Tierney (1991), noting the dearth of Native American faculty and staff in higher education, argues that non-Native staff and faculty must orient themselves to the concerns and issues of Native American students. Becoming more culturally aware regarding Native American people would allow non-Native faculty and staff to better serve Native American students and thus to be partner-colleagues for American Indian faculty and staff. The findings from McClellan's study (2003) involving new student affairs professionals in the Southwest suggest, however, that non-Native student affairs professionals may be poorly prepared to fulfill this role.

Working Together: A Personal Perspective

It has been my privilege to work in large public mainstream institutions of higher education with significant Native American student populations for approximately eighteen years as an administrator and faculty member. In addition, I have experienced firsthand what it is like to be a Comanche woman, raised in a tribal community, who attended day and boarding schools and earned degrees at predominantly white universities. My experiences and my cultural identity have influenced my perspective about higher education and my commitment to Native American students and issues.

Throughout my career I have worked with students from all backgrounds, including many Native American students. Over the years I have realized that many contemporary Native American students and I have common educational experiences, though we lived those experiences at different times and in different places. I can personally relate to feelings of isolation, cultural differences, and discrimination that often occur in our majority institutions of higher education. In addition, I can attest to the attitudes toward Native American faculty and staff that are present as individuals develop a career in these same institutions. Unfortunately, some of the same feelings and issues that confront Native Americans as students will continue to confront them in their professional life.

Difference, whether of color or other characteristics, is not always appreciated or accepted. Stereotypes abound in our society, and popular culture and the mass media reinforce them. This is certainly the case with Native American cultures and peoples. People of the majority culture often associate Native Americans with the past or with powwows, arts and crafts, and romantic images. The reality for contemporary Native American students is that they live in a global society and must develop skills and abilities that will prepare them for life in two worlds, Native American and non-Native. This development is manageable, though not without conflict and stress, because many Native American students have spent much of their lives negotiating between those two worlds.

The problems and issues that Native American students face at mainstream predominantly white institutions will not disappear overnight; and admitting, retaining, and graduating Native American students will take cooperative efforts by all faculty, staff, and administrators. In order to do this, institutional climates and attitudes must change. My experience says this starts at the top. If the university or college president and provost are committed to diversity, the chances of it happening in that institution increase. Yet resistance does exist, and change happens in small steps.

Professors and student affairs professionals are in advantageous positions to reach out to Native American students by providing academic support such as advising, mentoring, and maintaining a respectful classroom climate to help create an institution in which diversity is more than a word. These professionals who work with students, including Native American students, have the opportunity to implement respect, relevance, reciprocity, and responsibility, as Kirkness and Barnhardt advocate (1991).

The challenges are great but not impossible. Over my tenure in higher education, I have seen some positive changes. I continue to be optimistic about the future of having more Native American students in mainstream institutions succeeding academically. With increasing numbers of Native American students, faculty, and staff, institutions of higher education will become more diversified and a better place for all to study regardless of their background.

Having Native American faculty and staff along with academic and support programs helps attract, retain, and graduate students who are Native American. The existence of support services for Native American students contributes significantly to their academic success (Reyhner and Dodd, 1995). Because most professional staff in student affairs are non-Native, it is important for these individuals to have a working knowledge of Native American students. Non-Native faculty and staff who support and show an interest are critical for Native American students in mainstream higher education (Falk and Aitken, 1984). The question becomes: How can non-Native student affairs personnel and faculty begin to work with Native American faculty and staff who can assist them in making mainstream institutions of higher education more welcoming to Native American students?

Recommendations

Based on my experience as a Native American faculty member and administrator, I offer the following recommendations for non-Native student affairs professionals and faculty:

• *Network with Native American faculty and staff on campus.* Listening to and learning from Native Americans can be valuable to understanding Native American students and cultures. Because of the diversity in Native American cultures, do not expect Native American faculty and staff to be able to speak for all Native Americans, although they can become resources through recommending appropriate readings and serving on committees (university service is required of faculty members). Beware, however, of the overwhelming demands that mainstream institutions often place on American Indian faculty and staff (Kidwell, 1990; Stein, 1996). It is important to be reasonable and considerate of demands on Native American faculty and staff because they also have department and program responsibilities. However, in most cases Native American faculty and staff want to help Native American students succeed in higher education.

• *Learn something about Native American students attending your institution and the tribal nations they represent.* Seek out historical information about Native Americans. Understand the unique political and social status of tribes. Visit local Native American communities and nations as appropriate, and learn about contemporary issues of importance.

• *Do not generalize about Native Americans or promote stereotypes in your classrooms or programs.* Defuse stereotypes as much as possible; be sensitive and respectful of different ways of looking at things; and do not be judgmental or quick to assume. The mass media still misrepresents Native Americans, and this can lead to individuals making inappropriate comments (Tierney, 1991). Have patience and understanding, and help students in your classes and programs to do the same.

• *Become familiar with the support services for Native American students on your campus.* Get acquainted with the staff that works in these areas. Mentor or advise a Native American student. Encourage Native American students to come to office hours, and make them welcome. Do not pass off Native American students to Native American student affairs instead of working with them.

• *Use the resources of Native American studies programs.* If your university or a neighboring one has a Native American studies program, you have an enhanced opportunity to learn about tribal peoples. Attend some classes and public and department lectures and activities. Make appointments to visit with the department chair or Native American faculty and staff. Ask about possible internships for Native American studies majors to work in your program or research project. Native American studies majors have sound knowledge about Native American peoples and can be a resource. In addition, ask Native American studies faculty and staff to lecture or conduct workshops for student affairs personnel and non-Native faculty. Native American faculty and staff at majority institutions attract Native American students to their classes and often become mentors and advisers to them as a result. These Native American faculty members then become valuable resources to student affairs. Collaborate with Native American studies programs to cross list courses or develop joint degrees. Partner with Native American faculty and staff on research projects or scholarship.

• *Hire and promote Native American faculty and staff in all areas of the institution.* The presence of Native American faculty and staff will draw more students who are Native American to campus and help to diversify the institution. Hiring Native Americans into entry-level and senior positions is a strong sign to Native American communities and tribes of the institution's commitment to serving Native American students. The institution must give attention to the professional development and retention of Native American faculty and staff, augmenting it with collaborative partnerships with regional and professional associations.

• *Do not assume that mainstream teaching methods are appropriate for Native American students.* The Native American experience is unique; and Native American viewpoints, beliefs, and learning styles are often in conflict with the dominant society. Use a variety of teaching strategies and methods in your classroom to reach all learning styles.

• *Encourage academic disciplines in your institution to recruit and admit Native Americans into their degree programs.* Encourage Native American students to work in higher education as faculty and staff. Provide internship opportunities in your programs and departments so that students can get firsthand experience. Encourage Native Americans students, faculty, and staff to participate in professional organizations and to present or co-present at conferences.

• *Integrate more Native American content in curriculum and programming.* Address Native American students as a permanent part of orientation programs for students, staff, and faculty and include Native American parents as part of retention efforts. Where appropriate, include Native Americans in the course content. Native American history (past and present) is also the history of the United States.

• *Partner with tribal colleges and Native American organizations.* If your institution does not have Native American faculty or staff, collaborate and develop relationships with the nearest tribal college, institution of higher education with Native American faculty and staff, or Native American education organizations (for example, the American Indian Science and Engineering Society, the American Indian Graduate Center, the National Indian Education Association, and the National Institute for Native Leadership in Higher Education). Also, encourage non-Native professional organizations such as the National Association of Student Personnel Administrators and the American College Personnel Association to address Native American issues in higher education and to seek participation by Native American faculty and staff.

• *Place value on diversity in action as well as words.* Seek assistance from the institution's diversity committees, action plan, or Native American advisory board (if one exists). Having Native American faculty and staff serve on committees or task forces in your departments or programs will often bring a different perspective, enriching programming for Native American and non-Native students. Listening to and acting on the recommendations of Native American faculty and staff on committees and task forces will validate your commitment to diversity as being more than words.

• *Promote research.* Research is needed to explore a number of unanswered questions. Among these questions are the following:

Do the interactions between Native American staff or faculty and Native American students in majority higher education affect academic success?
What best practices exist for collaborative efforts between Native American and non-Native staff and faculty to support the success of Native American students?
What impact does the Native American studies program have on recruitment, retention, and graduation of Native American students and on their selection of a major or minor?

What impact does having Native American viewpoints and contributions integrated into the curriculum throughout the disciplines, not just in Native American studies, have on the academic success of Native American students and on the learning of all students?

Conclusion

The role that Native American faculty and staff can play in supporting Native American students and collaborating with non-Native faculty and staff in supporting the academic success of these students in higher education (both public and private) is an area that needs study. Little scholarship exists on the topic, and researchers have many questions to explore. The presence of Native American faculty and staff on majority campuses provides a unique opportunity for non-Native student affairs professionals and faculty to seek advisement, gain guidance, and develop collaborative efforts to better serve Native American students and their communities. Taking advantage of such opportunities can enrich the college experience; make the campus climate more welcoming for all students, Native American and non-Native; and promote diversity. As Wright (1987, p. 16) states, "A racially naïve or insensitive campus environment, one that is non-accepting of minority students' cultural and racial distinctiveness, can thwart or stifle development."

References

Bergstrom, A., Cleary, L. M., and Peacock, T. D. *The Seventh Generation: Native Students Speak About Finding the Good Path.* Charleston, W.Va.: ERIC Clearinghouse on Rural Education and Small Schools, 2003.

Brown L. L., and Kurpius Robinson, S. E. "Psychosocial Factors Influencing Academic Persistence of American Indian College Students." *Journal of College Student Development,* 1997, *38*(1), 3–12.

Cook-Lynn, E. *Why I Can't Read Wallace Stegner and Other Essays.* Madison: University of Wisconsin Press, 1996.

Cross, W. T. "Pathway to the Professorate: The American Indian Faculty Pipeline." *Journal of American Indian Education,* 1991, *30*(2), 13–24.

Falk, D., and Aitken, L. P. "Promoting Retention Among American Indian College Students." *Journal of American Indian Education,* 1984, *23*(2), 24–31.

Harvey, W. B. *Minorities in Higher Education 2001–2002: Nineteenth Annual Status Report.* Washington, D.C.: American Council on Education, 2002.

Hornett, D. "The Role of Faculty in Cultural Awareness and Retention of American Indian College Students." *Journal of American Indian Education,* 1989, *29*(1), 12–18.

Jackson, A. P., Smith, S. A., and Hill, C. L. "Academic Persistence Among Native American College Students." *Journal of College Student Development,* 2003, *44*(4), 548–565.

Kidwell, C. S. "Indian Professionals in Academe: Demand and Burnout." In *Opening the Montana Pipeline* (Proceedings from the American Indian Higher Education in the Nineties conference held in Bozeman, Mont.). Sacramento, Calif.: Tribal College Press, 1990.

Kirkness, V. J., and Barnhardt, R. "First Nations and Higher Education: The Four R's—Respect, Relevance, Reciprocity, and Responsibility." *Journal of American Indian Education*, 1991, *30*(3), 1–15.

Lin, R., LaCounte, D., and Eder, J. "A Study of Native American Students in a Predominantly White College." *Journal of American Indian Education*, 1988, 27(3), 8–15.

McClellan, G. S. "Multiculturalism as a 'Technology of Othering': An Exploratory Study of the Social Construction of Native Americans by Student Affairs Professionals in the Southwest." Doctoral dissertation, University of Arizona, 2003. Abstract in *Dissertation Abstracts International, 64,* 05A.

National Center for Education Statistics. *Digest of Educational Statistics, 2001.* Washington, D.C.: U.S. Department of Education, 2001a. http://nces.ed.gov/pubs2002/digest2001/tables/dt208.asp. Accessed Jan. 3, 2002.

National Center for Education Statistics. *Digest of Educational Statistics, 2001.* Washington, D.C.: U.S. Department of Education, 2001b. http://nces.ed.gov/pubs2002/digest2001/tables/dt207.asp. Accessed Jan. 3, 2002.

Ness, J. E. "American Indian Completers and Non-Completers in a Tribal College." *Tribal College Journal,* 2002, *13*(4), 36–40.

Pascarella, E. T., and Terenzini, P. T. *How College Affects Students: Findings and Insights from Twenty Years of Research.* San Francisco: Jossey-Bass, 1991.

Pavel, D. M., and Padilla, R. V. "American Indian and Alaska Native Postsecondary Departure: An Example of Assessing a Mainstream Model Using National Longitudinal Data." *Journal of American Indian Education*, 1993, 32(2), 1–23.

Reyhner, J., and Dodd, J. "Factors Affecting the Retention of American Indian and Alaska Native Students in Higher Education." Paper presented at the first annual conference of Expanding Minority Opportunities, Tempe, Ariz., Jan. 1995.

Stein, W. J. "The Survival of American Indian Faculty." In C. Turner, M. Garcia, A. Nora, and L. I. Rendón (eds.), *Racial and Ethnic Diversity in Higher Education* (ASHE Reader Series). Boston: Pearson Custom Publishing, 1996.

Stein, W. J. "Developmental Action for Implementing an Indigenous College: Philosophical Foundations and Pragmatic Steps." In M.K.P. Benham and W. J. Stein (eds.), *The Renaissance of American Indian Higher Education: Capturing the Dream* (pp. 25–59). Mahwah, N.J.: Lawrence Erlbaum Associates, 2003.

Swisher, K., Hoisch, M., and Pavel, D. M. *American Indian/Alaska Natives Dropout Study, 1991.* Washington D.C.: National Education Association, 1991.

Swisher, K. G., and Tippeconnic, J. W., III. "Research to Support Improved Practice in Indian Education." In K. G. Swisher and J. W. Tippeconnic III (eds.), *Next Steps: Research and Practice to Advance Indian Education.* Charleston, W.Va.: ERIC Clearinghouse on Rural Education and Small Schools, 1999.

Terenzini, P. T., Pascarella, E. T., and Blimling, G. "Students' Out-of-Class Experiences and Their Influence on Learning and Cognitive Development: A Literature Review." *Journal of College Student Development*, 1996, 37(2), 149–162.

Tierney, W. G. "Native Voices in Academe." *Change*, 1991, 23(2), 36–45.

Tierney, W. G. *Official Encouragement, Institutional Discouragement: Minorities in Academe—The Native American Experience.* Norwood, N.J.: Ablex, 1992.

Tierney, W. G. "Addressing Failure: Factors Affecting Native American College Retention." *Journal of Navajo Education*, 1995, *13*(1), 3–7.

Tippeconnic, J. W., and McKinney, S. "Native Faculty: Scholarship and Development." In M.K.P. Benham and W. J. Stein (eds.), *The Renaissance of American Indian Higher Education: Capturing the Dream.* Mahwah, N.J.: Erlbaum, 2003.

Verdugo, R. R. "Racial Stratification and the Use of Hispanic Faculty as Role Models: Theory, Policy, and Practice." *Journal of Higher Education*, 1995, 66(6), 669–693.

Wilson, P. "Key Factors in the Performance and Achievement of Minority Students at the University of Alaska, Fairbanks." *American Indian Quarterly,* 1998, 21(3), 535–545.

Wright, D. J. "Minority Students: Developmental Beginning." In D. J. Wright (ed.), *Responding to the Needs of Today's Minority Students* (pp. 5–21). New Directions for Student Services, no. 38. San Francisco: Jossey-Bass, 1987.

DR. MARY JO TIPPECONNIC FOX (COMANCHE) *is chair of American Indian Studies and ambassador to the Indian nations at the University of Arizona.*

Many issues and elements—including ethnic nomenclature, racial attitudes, and the legal and political status of American Indian nations and Indian people— influence Native American identity.

Native American Identity

Perry G. Horse (Kiowa)

"Some day we're all going to be like white people," my grandmother said in 1950. She noticed that the young people chose not to speak our native Kiowa language. She commented on the change in our diet from traditional foods to prepackaged goods. Popular American culture became dominant in daily life. More Kiowas were intermarrying with whites and into other tribes. Fifty-four years later I look around and think we may not be white people but indeed we are more like them. We emulate their ways. We are educated in their schooling system. We can speak and write like them. We have adopted their form of government. We perform their dance and music. We hold jobs and make mortgage and car payments. We are consumers. We enjoy the comforts of modern life. We attend mainstream universities. In many ways we have assimilated into the dominant culture. On the surface it seems we are indeed like them.

Be that as it may, we are still the original Native people of North America. We are Kiowa, Navajo, Comanche, Apache, Wichita, and so on down the list of five hundred or more Indian tribes. We cling to that distinction consciously and unconsciously. That realization, that consciousness, is where Native American identity begins. As Native American people we inherit an innate sensibility about the world that originated far back in our ancestral past. That consciousness, that psychology if you will, developed separately and apart from the experience of other peoples who were not indigenous to this land. It is a worldview that is inherent in Native American tribal traditions, most of which were handed down orally in the tribal languages.

Native American identity is multifaceted. Many issues or elements (such as ethnic nomenclature, racial attitudes, the legal and political status of American Indian nations and American Indian people, cultural change, and one's sensibility about what being a Native American means in today's society) influence Native American identity. In this chapter I share some insights about these issues and elements. Such insights are informed by my own experience and from interaction with Native American people of all backgrounds in Indian country.[1] I will then summarize how student affairs professionals may be able to use this information when working with students who are Native American.

Ethnic Nomenclature

American Indian, Indian, or Native American—which is it? My generation, those born just ahead of the so-called baby boomers, grew up American Indian. That is, we became accustomed to identifying with the ethnic descriptor *American Indian*. As a generic descriptor, it was convenient and readily recognizable. All the major organizations that dealt with Indian issues carried that designation. The U.S. Bureau of Indian Affairs is one example. The U.S. Indian Health Service is another. It was not just agencies of the U.S. government but also the National Congress of American Indians, the American Indian Higher Education Consortium, and the American Indian College Fund. American Indian studies departments in various universities were another example of organizations that preferred to use the designation of *American Indian*. So is it simply a matter of preference whether one uses *American Indian* or *Native American* in one's identity equation? Does it really matter?

I do not argue for one over the other. All I know is that when I hear the term *American Indian*, I immediately think of people like myself who are citizens of America's indigenous nations. When I hear the term *Native American*, I pause ever so slightly. I know that term includes me because I was born in this country, and I am an American citizen by dint of the Indian Citizenship Act of 1924. I know too that anyone born in this country can rightfully claim to be a native American.

What we are dealing with here are the peculiarities of linguistic meaning. There is a great deal of arbitrariness in the meanings associated with words. That is, the connection we associate with particular words is not an a priori connection. Rather, it is through agreement and usage among speakers of a given language that words acquire their meaning. So if we all agree to substitute *Native American* for *American Indian,* or to use the terms interchangeably, then we make a meaningful connection. Aside from that, it seems to be largely a matter of preference.

Racial Attitudes

In the past seven years, I have attended four national conferences on ethnicity, race, and identity.[2] Of the dozens of topics, workshops, and keynote speakers, the one that stands out in my mind dealt with the notion of white privilege. That term grew out of the identity movement in the late twentieth century. Those who coined the term were white scholars who approached ethnic studies by looking in the mirror to examine closely what it really means to be white in America. It was their attempt to understand and explain how race and racism in the United States affected white people.

Why should the study of whiteness be of interest to non-whites? To me, it goes to the matter of root cause. For American Indians, it puts a racial face on anti-Indian ideas such as manifest destiny. More to the point of our discussion, it sets the stage for a better understanding of our need for American Indian identity in the first place.

Jensen (1998, p. C1) has noted that "White privilege, like any social phenomenon, is complex. In a White supremacist culture, all White people have privilege, whether or not they are overtly racist themselves. There are general patterns, but such privilege plays out differently depending on context and other aspects of one's identity." Moreover, he points out that such privilege is unearned. Merely being white is sufficient in a world run mostly by white people.

White privilege is synonymous with dominance in a racially stratified society that is based on oppression. Any form of oppression, such as racism or sexism, is a relationship between a dominant, powerful group and a subordinated or oppressed group. To be white in such a society is to be privileged. All others are then underprivileged by definition, or so it would seem.

If we accept that American Indians have been or are oppressed, part of our identity is already subordinated. We consciously or unconsciously take on the characteristics of the oppressors. We favor the speaking of their language over our own Native American languages. We adopt their religious beliefs and practices. We emulate their forms of government and schooling. Some might say this is merely adaptive behavior for the sake of survival. Others would say it is part of a natural cycle of change.

Legal and Political Status

The legal and political status of American Indians in this country is what truly sets Indians apart from other U.S. citizens. The commerce clause of the U.S. Constitution authorizes the government to conduct business with American Indian nations on a government-to-government basis. Treaties between the United States and tribes remain in effect, and current federal American Indian policy acknowledges the sovereign status of tribal governments.

Under tribal sovereignty, tribal governments are the sole authority that can determine who is or is not a member, or citizen, of a given tribal nation. Each tribe maintains enrollment records. Thus if one seeks legal status as an American Indian, one must obtain tribal recognition as such. In the American Indian world, it is common to identify first with one's tribal affiliation and secondarily as American Indian or Native American. Within the tribe one's recognition is validated in various ways: parentage, clan relationships, kinship patterns, descendant status, one's individual tribal name, and other community-based norms. Merely declaring oneself to be American Indian without any of these will be transparent to those with authentic status as American Indian or tribal people.

I feel I am Kiowa because I have direct experience as such, including competence in speaking and understanding the language. On the other hand, if the Kiowa Business Council decided to remove me from the tribal rolls, I would lose my legal status as a tribal citizen. Although I like to think that this would be highly unlikely, it underscores an important point in the American Indian identity equation. Tribal governments, not individuals, determine one's legal status as an American Indian. This is important because tribal governments also have the power, if they so choose, to do away with the current identity benchmark of blood quantum.

I doubt that there is such a thing as degree of Indianness. Yet the federal government introduced the idea of degree of American Indian blood into our consciousness. The so-called Certificate of Indian Blood, which is necessary for obtaining certain forms of assistance, is an outgrowth of that proposition.[3] Legally, Indianness is a political proposition. It is a matter of citizenship in a given tribe. However, all tribes assess one's tribal membership eligibility based on blood quantum.

Non-Indians and American Indians alike sometimes misunderstand tribal sovereignty. Sovereignty is vested in the body politic of the tribe as a whole, not in individuals. Neither is sovereignty given or bestowed from one government to another. It is an inherent aspect of nationhood. Nations are free to recognize one another and to make treaties with one another. The United States has made treaties with American Indian tribes. Therefore, federal law recognizes those tribes as sovereign entities. It is at the state and local levels that tribal sovereignty is most often questioned or challenged in terms of jurisdictional disputes.

If tribal governments determine one's legal eligibility for recognition as an American Indian, or tribal member, then who recognizes the tribes? As we have already seen, tribes that made treaties with the United States are by virtue of those treaties federally recognized tribes. Also, state governments recognize some tribes. Interestingly, it is still possible for nonrecognized groups to petition for federal recognition as has happened recently in New England (see Benedict [2001] for further discussion). Although some observers claim that such groups may not "look Indian," those groups can attain tribal sovereignty with federal recognition and enjoy the same rights and benefits as other tribal nations.

Cultural Change

No culture or language remains static. Change is part of the natural order of things. American Indian cultures have changed and will continue to change over time. To be American Indian one hundred years ago would not be the same as being American Indian two hundred years ago. In 1803 American Indians in the West freely roamed and occupied their respective territories. By 1903 they were all confined to reservations. We America Indians look back in history and say about our ancestors, "Now, those were real American Indians." Project forward. Might the American Indians of the late twenty-second century say about today's American Indians, "Now, those were real American Indians"? Which leads to the question: What is a real American Indian? Does a static place in history mean anything? Most lay notions of Indianness are part American history, part myth, part ethnology, and part fiction.

Many American Indians feel that we should pay more attention to our own tribal teachings. Indeed, the proliferation of tribal colleges and universities is a manifestation of that concern. The American Indian colleges are also part of an American Indian response to being a colonized people. Where they exist, such colleges acknowledge cultural change while working to forestall further erosion of languages, culture, traditions, and so forth. Redefining what it means to be American Indian in today's society is one of the major issues in Indian country. Part of the American Indian redefinition process is driven, consciously or unconsciously, by the response of American Indians to white privilege.

Personal Sensibility

Ultimately, identity as an American Indian is highly personal. It is a particular way one feels about oneself and one's experience as an American Indian or tribal person. The principles or moral values that guide an individual's actions is that person's consciousness, and groups of people sharing common ethics can also be understood to have a collective consciousness. In an earlier essay (Horse, 2001), I described five influences on American Indian consciousness:

- The extent to which one is grounded in one's Native American language and culture, one's cultural identity
- The validity of one's American Indian genealogy
- The extent to which one holds a traditional American Indian general philosophy or worldview (emphasizing balance and harmony and drawing on Indian spirituality)
- One's self-concept as an American Indian
- One's enrollment (or lack of it) in a tribe

Although there are many threats to cultural transmission for American Indian people (popular press, stereotypes, and so on), I believe that the emergence of American Indian political and economic strength is contributing to the development of an American Indian postcolonial sensibility that is in turn helping support the growth of a renewed American Indian consciousness.

What Are You Anyway?

Those whose ethnic makeup is multicultural often express perplexity, if not frustration, when discussing their racial identity. At the aforementioned identity conferences, such individuals seemed resigned to their situation. However, they also expressed anger that they tend to be singled out with a common question: "What are you anyway?" If one does not clearly exhibit the physical characteristics of a single race, people seem compelled to confront such a person with that question. We should not be surprised that such is the case in a race-conscious society. According to Wijeyesinghe (2001), a key factor for multiracial people is whether they choose their racial identity themselves or whether they allow society or others to assign an identity to them.

Intertribal multicultural persons (American Indians of several tribal combinations) have a somewhat different situation in that they (or their parents) must choose in which tribe to enroll. In addition to the political aspect, such choice can have cultural and economic implications. In actual practice it is usually the parents who must choose. I know from personal experience that this is not easy. The issue is compounded when multitribal persons marry into an entirely different racial group.

Summary

The title of this essay is "Native American Identity," yet there is no standard descriptor, or nomenclature, for identifying those who call themselves American Indian or Native American. The terms are used interchangeably and seem to be based on preference. Those born before 1950 tend to be comfortable with being called American Indian. Those born later in the twentieth century seem accustomed to the term *Native American*. Readers should note that *Native American* now includes the indigenous people of Alaska, Hawaii, and American Samoa.

American society is racially stratified. White privilege, as white scholars put it, is synonymous with dominance in a white majority society and is based on oppression. All whites, whether or not they are overtly racist, benefit from white privilege. American Indian people struggle to maintain their own identity amid the pressures of adapting to and living in a white-dominated society.

Colonialism is a powerful force that affected American Indian cultures in many ways. However, no culture remains static. In fact, there is much cultural ambiguity among American Indians. In some communities the American Indian response to cultural change has been a deliberate return to traditional tribal knowledge, language, and practices. The establishment of tribal colleges and universities manifests part of that response. Christianity too has played a significant role in cultural change among Native Americans.

There is no such thing as a monolithic American Indian entity. Tribes and American Indian nations are bewildering in their diversity. Yet non-Indians tend to think and act otherwise. One's identity as an American Indian is highly personal. American Indians share some commonalities in terms of social interactions and certain pan-Indian cultural activities such as modern-day intertribal celebrations. However, the practical benchmark for Indianness is the political distinction that tribes enjoy as sovereign nations. Members of tribal nations are thus dual citizens. They are citizens of the United States and of their respective tribal nations. It is not simply a matter of American Indians being just another ethnic minority.

Recommendations

Existing theories and models of racial identity have limitations and strengths. Those who work with Native American students need to keep in mind that American Indian or tribal identity is a personalized process that is influenced by legal and political considerations, psychosocial factors, proximity or access to a given culture, socialization, and one's own sensibility. Models of racial identity proliferated in the 1980s and 1990s, but few have focused on identity development among Indians. I discuss some psychosocial influences on American Indian identity in my 2001 essay, but it is not an identity model as such.

Administrators, teachers, and higher education practitioners who interact professionally with Native American students can assess themselves in terms of their reaction to each of the major points in this essay. If the reader feels challenged by these assertions, that may be a signal to rethink the way one feels, especially about the points on racism and white privilege. With regard to the latter, simply typing in these keywords on any Internet search engine will reveal numerous sources of information, essays, and articles.

Many mainstream colleges and universities now have departments of American Indian studies or something similar. Staff people in such organizations can provide further guidance around Native identity and related issues.

Over a half century has passed since my grandmother lamented the idea of American Indians becoming like white people. Indeed, we now see more evidence of cultural assimilation among American Indians. But that is not the same as identity. Identity, our sense of who we really are, lies in the self-image inherited from our ancestors and passed down along a tribal memory chain. So long as that memory chain remains unbroken, we can stay connected to what our elders called the tribal spirit force. May it always be so!

Notes

1. The term *Indian country* is most usefully defined as "country within which Indian laws and customs and federal laws relating to Indians are generally applicable" (Cohen, 1942, p. 5). This definition includes all territory owned or controlled by Native Americans and Alaska Natives.

2. The Southwest Center for Human Relations, University of Oklahoma, sponsors the annual National Conference on Race and Ethnicity in Higher Education at different regional locations.

3. The Department of the Interior, Bureau of Indian Affairs (BIA), issues the Certificate of Indian Blood; this important document attests to one's degree of American Indian blood and one's membership in a given tribal nation. It is issued based on the records of the BIA field offices that in turn verify one's tribal membership with the tribe concerned.

References

Benedict, J. *Without Reservation: How a Controversial Indian Tribe Rose to Power and Built the World's Largest Casino.* New York: Perennial, 2001.

Cohen, F. S. *Handbook of Federal Indian Law.* Albuquerque: University of New Mexico Press, 1942.

Horse, P. G. "Reflections on American Indian Identity." In C. L. Wijeyesinghe and B. W. Jackson III (eds.), *New Perspectives on Racial Identity Development: A Theoretical and Practical Anthology.* New York: New York University Press, 2001.

Jensen, R. "White Privilege Shapes the U.S." *Baltimore Sun,* July 19, 1998. http://www.baltimoresun.com. Accessed Feb. 12, 2004.

Wijeyesinghe, C. L. "Racial Identity in Multiracial People: An Alternative Paradigm." In C. L. Wijeyesinghe and B. W. Jackson III (eds.), *New Perspectives on Racial Identity Development: A Theoretical and Practical Anthology.* New York: New York University Press, 2001.

DR. PERRY G. HORSE (KIOWA) *serves as consultant to tribal colleges and on Native American higher education issues.*

*This chapter provides general insights into American
Indian epistemologies that can assist student affairs
professionals in their work and examines the shared
understandings of American Indians with regard to tribal
knowledge and education.*

American Indian Epistemologies

Gregory A. Cajete (Tewa)

This chapter explores a vision of American Indian education and epistemologies, which unfold through the tracking of a very special story. It is an
honoring of a process for seeking life that American Indian people represent and reflect through their special connections to nature, family, community, and spiritual ecology. It is an honoring of relationships and the
place that traditional teaching and learning have in American Indian life.
This chapter maps a journey through shared metaphors, making various
stops to recognize, appreciate, and contemplate traditional American Indian
epistemologies and implications for the future of American Indian children
and the tribal cultures that they will carry into the twenty-first century.

Education from an American Indian Perspective

There is no word for *epistemology* in any American Indian language.
However, there is certainly a body of understandings that can be said to
include what this branch of Western philosophy would explore as the ori-
gins, nature, and methods of coming to know a way of life (Deloria, 1973;
Deloria and Wildcat, 2001; Kawagley, 1995; Peat, 1996; Suzuki and
Knudtson, 1992; Waters, 2004). Indeed, one might say that there are as
many American Indian epistemologies as there are American Indian tribes.
To understand the nature of American Indian epistemologies, it is useful to
explore the realm of cultural ideals from which the learning, teaching, and
systems of education of Native America evolved.

American Indian education historically occurred in a holistic social
context that developed a sense of the importance of each individual as a
contributing member of the social group. Essentially, tribal education

worked as a cultural and life-sustaining process. It was a process of education that unfolded through reciprocal relationships between one's social group and the natural world. This relationship involved all dimensions of one's being while providing both personal development and technical skills through participation in the life of the community. It was essentially an integrated expression of environmental education.

Understanding the depth of relationships and the significance of participation in all aspects of life are the keys to traditional American Indian education. *Mitakuye Oyasin* (we are all related) is a Lakota phrase that captures an essence of tribal education because it reflects the understanding that our lives are truly and profoundly connected to other people and the physical world. Likewise, in tribal education one gains knowledge from firsthand experience in the world and then transmits or explores it through ritual, ceremony, art, and appropriate technology. The individual then uses knowledge gained through these vehicles in the context of everyday living. Education in this context becomes education for life's sake. Indigenous education is at its very essence learning about life through participation and relationship to community, including not only people but plants, animals, and the whole of nature (Cajete, 1994).

Elemental Points About Indigenous Education

A number of elements characterize indigenous education and processes. These elements characterize the expression of indigenous education wherever and however it has been expressed. These elements are like the living stones, the *Inyan* as the Lakota term it, that animate the expressions of indigenous education. A few of these characteristics are included here to provide landmarks to assist the reader (Cajete, 1994).

The sacred view of Nature permeates and contextualizes the foundational process of teaching and learning.

Integration and interconnectedness are universal traits.

Relationships between elements and knowledge bases radiate in concentric rings of process and structure.

Its processes adhere to the principle of reciprocity between humans and all other things.

It recognizes and incorporates the cycles within cycles, that is, that there are always deeper levels of meaning to be found in every learning-teaching process.

It presents something to learn for everyone, at every stage of life.

It recognizes the levels of maturity and readiness to learn in the developmental process of both males and females. This recognition is incorporated into the designs and situations in which indigenous teaching takes place.

It recognizes language as a sacred expression of breath and incorporates this orientation in all its foundations.

It recognizes that each person and each culture contain the seeds of all that are essential to their well-being and positive development.

It recognizes and applies ordering through ceremony, ritual, and community activity.

It recognizes that the true sources of knowledge are to be found within the individual and entities of nature.

It recognizes that true learning occurs through participating in and honoring relationships in both the human and natural communities.

It recognizes the power of thought and language to create the worlds we live in.

It creates maps of the world that assist us through our life's journey.

It resonates and builds learning through the tribal structures of the home and community.

Finding Face, Finding Heart, and Finding a Foundation

The characteristics of American Indian epistemologies reflect traits that indigenous cultures of the world share. They are really expressions of the ancestral tribal roots of all the families of humankind. In exploring the tribal foundations of American Indian education, we are really tracking the earliest sources of human teaching and learning. What these foundations have to teach us is that learning is ultimately a subjective experience tied to a place: environmentally, socially, and spiritually. Tribal teaching and learning was intertwined with the daily life of both teacher and learner. Tribal education was a natural outcome of living in close communion with each other and the natural environment.

The living place, the learner's extended family, the clan and tribe provide both the context and source for teaching. In this way every situation provided a potential opportunity for learning; and basic education was not separate from the natural, social, or spiritual aspects of everyday life. Living and learning were fully integrated.

The ideals of such a process naturally became founded on the continuous development of self-knowledge, on finding life through understanding and participating in the creative process of living, on direct awareness of the natural environment, on knowledge of one's role and responsibility to community, and on cultivating a sensitivity to the spiritual essences of the world. To attain such ideals required participation in a shared cultural metaphor and the continuity of knowledge, perception, experience, and wisdom that the understanding and experience of tribal elders afforded.

The cultivation of all one's senses through learning how to listen, observe, and experience holistically by creative exploration was highly valued. In addition, all tribes highly regarded the ability to use language through storytelling, oratory, and song as a primary tool for teaching and learning. This was because the spoken or sung word expressed the spirit and breath of life of the speaker and thus was considered sacred.

A quality of informality characterized the greater part of American Indian teaching and learning, because most traditional knowledge was contextualized in the day-to-day life experience of the people. However, formal learning was almost always required in the transfer of sacred knowledge. Therefore, various ceremonial practices formed a complex for the formal teaching and learning of sacred knowledge that was founded on experience and participation in a tribal culture. Initiation rites occurred at graduated stages of growth and maturation. Important initiation ceremonies and accompanying forms of formal education were integrated with the natural physical and psychological transitions occurring at the end of early childhood; puberty; early, middle, and late adulthood; and old age. Ceremony was a lifelong process of introduction to sacred and environmental knowledge, graduated and programmed in such a way that individuals were presented new levels of knowledge when they were physically, psychologically, and socially ready to learn them.

Hah oh is a Tewa phrase sometimes used to connote the process of learning. Its literal translation is to breathe in. *Hah oh* is an Indian metaphor that describes the perception of traditional tribal education—a process of breathing in—that each tribe creatively and ingeniously applied. As a whole, traditional tribal education revolved around experiential learning (learning by doing or seeing), storytelling (learning by listening and imagination), ritual or ceremony (learning through initiation), dreaming (learning through unconscious imagery), the tutor (learning through apprenticeship), and artistic creation (learning through creative synthesis). These methods fully honored the integration of the inner and outer realities of learners and teachers, and they fully engaged the complementary educational processes of both realities (Cajete, 1994).

The legacy of the traditional forms of American Indian education are significant because they embody a quest for self, individual and community survival, and wholeness in the context of a community and natural environment. Indigenous education is really endogenous education; that is, it is an educating of the inner self through an enlivening and illumination from one's own being and the learning of key relationships. Therefore, the foundations for indigenous education naturally rest on increasing awareness and developing innate human potentials through time. Based on this orientation, American Indians and other indigenous groups used ritual, myth, customs, and life experience to integrate both the process and content of learning into the very fabric of their social organizations, thereby promoting wholeness in the individual, family, and community.

Foundations of Indigenous Epistemologies

Indians throughout the Americas incorporate a number of symbolic expressions that reflect the metaphysical, ecological, and cultural constructs of tribal epistemology. These symbolic constructs, when translated, include the following: Tree of Life, Earth Mother, Sun Father, Sacred Twins, Mother of Game or Corn, Old Man, Trickster, Holy Wind or Life's Sake, We Are All Related, Completed Man/Woman, the Great Mystery, Life Way, and Sacred Directions. These expressions, which occur in a variety of forms in nearly all American Indian languages, reflect common understandings and shared foundations for traditional ways of learning. That is, behind each of these mythic metaphors are the philosophical infrastructures and fields of tribal knowledge that lie at the heart of American Indian epistemologies. For instance, among the Iroquois, the Tree of Life and its white roots of peace form a rich matrix of interrelated myths that present not only Iroquoian traditional knowledge but truths that other tribes recognize. Likewise, the Iroquoian myth of the Great Turtle is an archetypal Earth Mother tale that embodies the understanding of the Whole Earth as a living, breathing, and knowing entity who nourishes and provides for every living thing through its own magnificent process of life. The Earth Mother's counterpart in maintaining life, the Sun Father, is represented in various key roles in such myths as Scar Face among the Blackfoot and the Old Man of the Crystal House among the Chumash (Wood, 1982).

These myths, and the variety of myths related to the other symbolic complexes mentioned, present the Nature-centered orientation of indigenous epistemologies in the Americas. Indeed, rightful orientation to the natural world is the primary message and intent of the mythic perception that the sacred directions symbolize among American Indians. The majority of American Indian tribes recognize seven sacred or elemental directions: East, West, North, South, Zenith, Nadir, and the Center. Through deep understanding and expression of the metaphoric meaning of these orientations, American Indians have intimately defined their place in the Universe.

By perceiving themselves in the middle of these directions, they oriented themselves to the multidimensional fields of knowledge and the phenomena of their physical and spiritual worlds. Individual tribes named each direction and associated symbols with the directions that characterized their perceptions and experiences with each. These symbols invariably included natural phenomena, colors, animals, plants, spirits, and holy winds (kinds of thought).

Seven Foundations of Tribal Education

Extending the metaphor of environmental orientation and process inherent in these sacred directions to education, we may speak of seven elemental yet highly integrated kinds of thought that form the foundations on which the vehicles and contexts of indigenous education rest (Cajete, 1994). These orienting foundations may include the Environmental, the Mythic, the Artistic, the Visionary, the Affective, the Communal, and the Spiritual. In traditional life these foundations are so intimately interrelated that they act relativistically at all levels of their expression. In every sense they contain each other in such a way that exploration of any one foundation can take you into the very heart of the tribal education experience. However, a complementary balance occurs in the interplay of these foundations. This balance can be illustrated by the interaction and interpretation of foundations that play within the environmental and spiritual fields of experience. An ebb and flow of interactive realities characterizes the play among these foundations of education.

Environmental Foundation. The Environmental foundation forms a context through which the tribe observed and integrated those understandings, bodies of knowledge, and practices resulting from direct interaction with the natural world. This foundation connects a tribe to its place, establishing the meaning of tribe members' relationships to their land and the earth in their minds and hearts. To say that American Indians were America's first practical ecologists is a gross simplification of a deep sense of ecological awareness and state of being. The environmental foundation of tribal education reflects a deeper level of teaching and learning than simply making a living from the natural world. For American Indians, as with other nature-centered indigenous cultures around the world, the natural environment was the essential reality, the place of being. Nature was taught about and understood in and on its own terms. Relationship and its expressions in all aspects of life formed the basis for a profound process of education.

Based on the environmental foundation of tribal education, tribal people and their environment established and perpetuated a mutual and reciprocal relationship. Nature was used for sustenance; however, the use of material technology was elegant, sophisticated, and appropriate within the context of traditional society (Cajete, 1994).

Mythic Foundation. The Mythic foundation rests on the archetypal stories that describe the cosmology in the language and cultural metaphors of a tribe. This foundation explores the guiding thoughts, dreams, explanations, and orientations to the world. In short, this foundation represents the tribe's worldview and, through the process and structure of storytelling, presents the script for teaching, learning, and participating in the stories that guide a people. Ultimately, all education is the expression of some sort of storytelling.

Visionary Foundation. The Visionary foundation rests on the deep psychological and spiritual experiences at the individual level that lead to or result from a tribe's practices, rituals, and ceremonies. Such practices and contexts provide a framework for individuals and groups to teach and learn through exploring their inner psychology and their collective unconscious. American Indians applied the visionary foundation to directly access knowledge and understanding from primary sources deep within themselves and in the natural world.

Artistic Foundation. The Artistic foundation contains the practices, mediums, and forms through which we usually express the meanings and understandings we have come to see. Art allows us to symbolize knowledge, understanding, and feelings through image, thus making it possible to transcend a finite time and cultural wrapping. Art itself becomes a primary source of teaching because it both integrates and documents a profound process of learning. Art was such an integral part of American Indian life that the various Indian languages have no words that translate exactly to mean Art. The closest direct translation to English refers to making or completing. The Artistic foundation also acts as a bridging and translating foundation for the Mythic and Visionary foundations. That is, the Artistic mediates the other two.

The Mythic, Visionary, and Artistic foundations form a natural triad of tools, practices, and ways of teaching and learning that, through their interaction and play, form a fourth dimension for deep understanding of our inner being. Remembering the metaphor of the Sacred Twins, we may say that this triad of foundations springs forth from the twin that represents the teaching, learning, and innate knowledge of our inner self. It might be called the Winter Twin or the deeply inward aspect of indigenous education.

Affective Foundation. The Affective foundation of tribal education forms a second context that contains the emotional response to learning, living, growing, and understanding in relationship to the world, ourselves, and each other. This is the foundation in which we establish rapport with what we are learning and why we are learning it. It reflects the whole gamut of our emotion as it relates to the educational process. It is the seat of our primary motivation and the way we establish personal or group meaning for our learning. It is the foundation through which we cultivate our intention, choice, trust, responsibility, and heart for learning. And like the Artistic foundation, the Affective foundation acts as a bridge between the environmental and communal foundations. It mediates our feelings for our place and our community. For American Indians love for one's land and people have always been a primary motivation for learning and service to one's tribe.

Communal Foundation. The Communal foundation forms a third context containing the responses and experiences that reflect the social and communal dimension of tribal education. The life of the community, as well as the individuals of that community, is the primary focus of tribal education. The community is also the primary context—through the family, clan, or other tribal social structures—in which the first dimensions of education unfold for all human beings. All humans after all are social animals who depend on each other directly not only for their mutual survival but their identity. The Communal experience is the seat of human cultures; as such, there is not one thing in human life that it does not influence. The Communal experience and the inherent process for teaching and learning in tribal cultures are tied through history and tradition to some of the oldest and most instinctually human-contexted mediums of education. The structure, process, and content of teaching and learning resulting from traditional American Indian tribal and communal experience were and continue to be inherently human, highly contexted, situational, highly flexible, and informal. Learning and teaching are going on at all times, at all levels, and in a variety of situations. For American Indian tribal education, the community was and continues to be the schoolhouse!

Spiritual Foundation. The Spiritual orientation of tribal education may be considered as both a foundational process and field through which traditional American Indian education occurs. For indigenous peoples Nature and all that it contains formed the parameters of the school. Each of the other foundations of tribal education are exquisitely complex and dynamic contexts through which a kind of thought develops from a unique yet creative process of teaching and learning. The Affective, Communal, and Environmental foundations form the other triad of tools, practices, and way of teaching and learning that complements the understanding of the first triad. This might be called the Summer Twin or the highly interactive and external dimension of indigenous education.

In traditional American Indian life, the context in which these foundations interact is the Spiritual-Ecological, the seventh orienting foundation of knowledge and process. It is the Spiritual that forms not only the foundation for religious expression but the ecological psychology that underpins the other foundations.

A value many American Indian people share is that they must preserve their stories, languages, customs, songs, dances, and ways of thinking and learning because they sustain the life of the individual, family, and community. The stories in particular integrate the life experience and reflect the essence of the people's sense of spiritual being through time and space. For the mythic stories of a people form the script for cultural processes and experience.

Culture is the face; myth is the heart; and traditional education is the foundation for indigenous life. And all cultures have indigenous roots that are bedded in the rich soil of myth from which the most elemental stories of human life spring.

Tewa Indian elders often admonish young people to live the myths by saying "these stories, this language, these ways, and this land are the only valuables we can give you—but life is in them for those who know how to ask and how to learn."

The metaphor for this seeking is coded in the Tewa phrase *pin peyé obe* (look to the mountain)! A first step in reconnecting contemporary American Indian education to its mythic roots begins with looking to the cardinal mountains of thought and perspective from which all the essences of our stories come and to which they return. For with or without our collective and conscious participation, a new story of education is beginning to emerge. Understanding the plot of this new story is a first task for forging an indigenous philosophy of American Indian education that will ensure cultural survival in the twenty-first century.

Final Thoughts

Environmental relationship, myth, visionary traditions, traditional arts, tribal community, and Nature-centered spirituality have traditionally formed the foundations of American Indian life. These elements formed a context for discovering one's true face (character, potential, identity), one's heart (soul, creative self, true passion), and one's foundation (true work, vocation), all of which lead to the expression of a complete life.

A primary orientation of indigenous education was that each person was in reality his or her own teacher and that learning was connected to each individual's life process. One looked for meaning in everything, especially in the workings of the natural world. All things of Nature were teachers of humankind; what was required was a cultivated and practiced openness to the lessons that the world had to teach. Ritual, mythology, and the art of storytelling combined with the cultivation of relationship to one's inner self; individuals used the family, the community, and the natural environment to help realize their potential for learning and a complete life. Individuals were enabled to reach completeness by being encouraged to learn how to trust their natural instincts, to listen, to look, to create, to reflect and see things deeply, to understand and apply their intuitive intelligence, and to recognize and honor the spirit within themselves and the natural world. This is the educational legacy of indigenous peoples. It is imperative that we revitalize its message and its way of educating for life's sake at this time of ecological crisis.

For American Indians a new circle of education is evolving that is founded on the roots of tribal education and reflective of the needs, values, and sociopolitical issues as Indian people themselves perceive them. This new circle encompasses the importance that American Indian people place on the continuance of their ancestral traditions. It emphasizes a respect for individual uniqueness in the diversity of expressions of spirituality, facilitates a more comprehensive understanding of history and culture, develops a strong sense of place and service to community, and forges a commitment to educational and social transformation that recognizes and further empowers the inherent strength of American Indian people and their respective cultures.

References

Cajete, G. A. *Look to the Mountain*. Durango, Colo.: Kivaki Press, 1994.

Deloria, V. *God Is Red*. New York: Dell, 1973.

Deloria, V., Jr., and Wildcat, D. R. *Power and Place: Indian Education in America*. Golden, Colo.: Fulcrum Resources, 2001.

Kawagley, A. O. *A Yupiaq Worldview: A Pathway to Ecology and Spirit*. Prospect Heights, Ill.: Waveland Press, 1995.

Peat, F. D. *Lighting the Seventh Fire: The Spiritual Ways, Healing, and Science of the Native American.* New York: Birch Lane Press, 1996.
Suzuki, D., and Knudtson, P. *Wisdom of the Elders.* New York: Bantam Press, 1992.
Waters, A. (ed.). *American Indian Thought.* Cambridge, Mass.: Blackwell, 2004.
Wood, M. *Spirits, Heroes, and Hunters from North American Mythology.* New York: Schocken Books, 1982.

DR. GREGORY A. CAJETE (TEWA) *is director of Native American studies and associate professor in Language, Literacy, and Socio-cultural studies at the University of New Mexico.*

This chapter discusses the ways in which tribal colleges have incorporated culturally relevant education models to serve American Indian students.

Serving American Indian Students in Tribal Colleges: Lessons for Mainstream Colleges

Robert G. Martin (Cherokee)

Culturally relevant programs can improve contemporary American Indian students' chances for academic success. Cultural relevancy has implications for curriculum, instruction (teaching methods adapted to students' learning styles), evaluation (not limited to standardized tests), and governance. Culturally relevant education existed among American Indian societies for centuries before European contact. Essential characteristics of this successful education were that it was holistic, relevant, participatory, and controlled by Indian people (Martin, 1994). Education, language, religion, and government were the social institutions that made American Indian communities thriving and distinct societies. Through the interaction of these institutions, communities maintained a strong sense of history and identity.

This chapter will discuss the ways in which tribal colleges have incorporated culturally relevant education models to serve American Indian students. Following this discussion the chapter will present potential strategies for increasing persistence rates for American Indian students at mainstream colleges and universities.

Tribal Colleges

If the number of American Indian students experiencing success in higher education is to increase significantly, colleges and universities must change their organization and structure in order to better meet the needs of an

NEW DIRECTIONS FOR STUDENT SERVICES, no. 109, Spring 2005 © Wiley Periodicals, Inc.

increasingly diverse student body (Tierney, 1992). One of the most significant developments in American Indian education since the 1970s has been
the establishment of the tribal colleges. Their impact on American Indian
students in higher education has been dramatic. They have positively
affected the participation, retention, and graduation rates of American
Indian students in higher education by providing programs and classes that
are more culturally sensitive and relevant to the unique needs of American
Indian students (Boyer, 1997). Tribal colleges have played a vital role in
providing higher education opportunities for American Indians by incor-
porating tribal-specific culture, history, and language into their academic
and student support programs.

In addition to offering culturally relevant education to American Indian
students, tribal colleges function as research centers for the study of culture,
cultural preservation, and economic development issues in American Indian
communities. Tribal colleges are deeply involved in a wide range of community efforts such as basic education, counseling services, and economic
development initiatives. They also offer courses in traditional subjects such
as tribal languages, which are crucial to preserving cultural identities
(American Indian College Fund [AICF], 2003).

The success of tribal colleges in serving American Indian students and
communities is remarkable when one considers the array of social and economic challenges confronting those students and communities. Among
these challenges are poverty and the associated lack of social services (Pavel,
1992), unemployment rates approaching 80 percent, extremely low high
school completion rates (American Indian Higher Education Consortium
[AIHEC], 1999), suicide rates more than double the national average,
extremely high incidences of alcohol-related accidents and deaths (O'Brien,
1992), and other major health concerns. Access to postsecondary institutions is more limited in American Indian communities. Tribal colleges must
at the very least consider all of these socioeconomic factors when formu-
lating educational strategies and programs.

Organization of Tribal Colleges

Tribally controlled colleges are chartered by sovereign tribal nations and
must maintain a board of directors that is exclusively or predominantly
American Indian (Stein, 1992). There are currently thirty-five tribally controlled colleges and universities in the United States, with more than a
dozen in the planning stages; and enrollments are increasing. All tribal colleges offer associate degrees. An increasing number offer bachelor's degrees,
and a few offer master's degrees. Most of the colleges are accredited by
regional accrediting agencies; the others are candidates for accreditation.

In most cases tribal colleges do not receive funds from the states in
which they are located (Matthews, 1999). Financial support for tribal colleges from the tribes and the communities they serve has been limited

because of the poor economic conditions on many reservations, though recent economic growth in some nations is improving funding for their tribal colleges. The federal government supplies most of the colleges' financial support under the Tribally Controlled College or University Assistance Act (Stein, 1999). Unfortunately, funding was less than $4,000 per student in 2003, which is 40 percent less than what the typical community college receives in per-student funding from federal, state, and local government revenues (AIHEC, 1999).

AIHEC was organized in 1972 to provide an opportunity for tribal college boards of directors, administration, faculty, and students to communicate and collaborate with one another to support the mission of tribal colleges. In 1978 AIHEC was successful in lobbying congress for the passage of the Tribally Controlled College Act, Public Law 92–471, which provides core funding for the colleges (Stein, 1992). It also successfully advocated for its member institutions to receive land-grant status from the United States Congress in 1994. This congressional action has assisted tribal colleges in enhancing and expanding curriculum related to agriculture, natural resources management, and engineering. In addition, after many years of hard work by the AIHEC leadership, President Clinton signed the Tribal College Executive Order in 1996. This executive order has increased the visibility and participation of the tribal colleges in federal programs (AIHEC, 1999).

Tribal College Students

In 1982 fewer than twenty-five hundred students were enrolled in tribal colleges. Today enrollment is more than thirty thousand students and rapidly growing (AICF, 2003). The growth in enrollment is occurring despite financial shortages, poor academic facilities, and service to an at-risk student population. The average age of tribal college students is twenty-eight; sixty-four percent are women; and a large percentage are single parents. Despite the high risk factors of many tribal college students, 86 percent persist to complete a degree. Moreover, after attending tribal colleges, American Indian student persistence rates at mainstream institutions are four times the rate of those for American Indian students who have never attended a tribal college (AICF, 2003).

Tribal colleges have greater success with American Indian students because they recognize the importance of individualized attention, offer programs that are culturally sensitive, and have learned that family support services are integral to their students' progress and success. Tribal colleges understand the importance of the student's role within his or her cultural, family, and community context (Boyer, 1997). Accordingly, tribal colleges value the role of family and community in their students' lives and provide for flexible policies that permit students to maintain their familial and tribal obligations. Close proximity to home community, personal attention, and culturally relevant curriculum are among the reasons students choose to enroll in tribal colleges (AICF, 2003).

Tribal and federal financial aid programs are often unable to address the economic situations of American Indian students (Stein, 2003). Tribal colleges have made financial aid assistance for their students a priority. More than 90 percent of American Indian students require financial aid (AICF, 2003). Tribal colleges provide financial aid programs to American Indian students from a variety of sources, including the tribe, federal, and state governments; benefactors; and private foundations. For example, scholarships from the AICF have played a crucial role in increasing persistence rates for tribal college students by allowing recipients to make their education a higher priority than work. Many of the scholarship recipients are able to reduce their work hours so that they can focus more on coursework (AICF, 2003).

Culturally Relevant Education Models

Extended families are an integral component of American Indian cultures. Family obligations can be so great that they can interfere with school. Families, however, also can be used to enhance academic and social integration for American Indian students. The Family Education Model (FEM) has been implemented at four tribal colleges in Montana to improve retention rates among tribal college students. FEM's family-centered approach builds on student and family strengths, offering strategies for increasing the student support network. Families are invited to participate in the college's cultural activities such as social dances, storytelling, and traditional arts and crafts (Ortiz and Heavyrunner, 2003).

American Indian cultural symbols reinforce identity and increase comfort levels for American Indian students. At most tribal colleges, the architectural design of campus buildings and landscaping reflect an American Indian motif. For example, the main campus of Diné College is located at the geographic center of the reservation, and the central administration building is constructed in the shape of a hogan, the Diné traditional home (Boyer, 1997). (See the Resources section of this volume for more information about tribal colleges.) At Tohono O'odham Community College, a *wato* (*ramada*) is the first structure that visitors see when they enter the campus. The *wato* is made with four tree trunks set in the ground to serve as the corners. Saguaro cactus ribs are tied between them on the ends and along the sides. Ocotillo branches are then laid over the saguaro ribs. The *wato* provides shade and shelter in the desert and is frequently used for social gatherings and ceremonies.

Another example is the four-acre medicine wheel that stands along the southern boundary of the campus at Haskell Indian Nations University (Haskell). The medicine wheel is symbolic of the worldview for many tribes, representing the four cardinal directions, the four aspects of our human nature, and the interconnection and relation of the entire natural world. The university's medicine wheel is located south of campus adjacent to the Haskell-Baker Wetlands and to sweat lodges; students, faculty, and community members all use it. The area is the focal point for campus cultural and spiritual activities (Low, 1994).

Tribal colleges have also implemented programs to assist American Indian students in making the transition from high school to college. For example, Haskell implemented summer bridge programs that bring high school students to campus for math and science enrichment programs. Also, the university established new student orientation programs and extended orientation courses. The new student orientation program is a one- or two-day experience offered during the summer for freshman students and their parents. Student evaluations revealed that two-day programs allow student participants to become better acquainted with other new students and with the institution.

Once students enter the tribal colleges, they experience culturally relevant academic and student support services that will enhance their opportunities for success. Haskell implemented a one-credit hour required course called Vision Quest–The Freshman Year Experience to provide an opportunity for students to learn more about American Indian culture. Vision Quest addresses retention, academic preparedness, and survival skills. The course is designed to be culturally relevant. Most tribes have the tradition of expecting a young person just before achieving adulthood to seek out a secluded spot to enter into a state of dreams and visions. At this time the individual discovers purpose and direction in life. The intent of Vision Quest is to serve as the academic parallel of self-discovery. The course seeks to provide the skills that students need for success in higher education and life.

Each student in Vision Quest must select a mentor. The mentor program is designed to encourage and allow faculty and staff to play a role in students' pursuit of education by acting as a resource, offering support, and participating in students' academic and personal development. The lack of mentors and role models in many American Indian communities who are able to convey that one can obtain a valuable education while maintaining one's cultural identity makes mentoring programs essential to the success of American Indian students (Ortiz and Heavyrunner, 2003).

Tribal colleges assist their graduating students in transferring to mainstream universities. Several years ago at Haskell's request, the University of Kansas (KU), implemented a mentoring program for students who transferred from the tribal college to KU. The goal was to improve the students' first-year experiences and increase their retention and graduation rates. The program included the following: early enrollment opportunity; faculty, student, and staff mentors; expanded orientation programs with staff from both KU and Haskell; and a textbook grant for participants. During the program's first year, all twenty-one students who had enrolled for the fall semester returned for the spring.

Haskell and KU also implemented a student exchange program whereby students at one institution enroll in the other and pay only their home institution's tuition. This has benefited students by permitting them to enroll in classes that their institution was unable to offer. For example, an American Indian studies student from Haskell was able to earn fifteen credit hours with a 4.0 grade point average in Russian studies at KU.

There has been an increase in both higher education enrollment and completion rates for American Indians since the 1970s. Moreover, American Indian enrollment has shifted from two-year colleges to four-year colleges. Obviously, tribal colleges have played a major role in the growing number of American Indians who are accessing and finding success in higher education (Ortiz and Heavyrunner, 2003).

Recommendations

Tribal colleges have improved participation and persistence rates of American Indian students by creating culturally relevant learning environments more conducive to the students' success. If mainstream colleges and universities are to replicate this success, then they must be committed to increasing academic and social integration by establishing administrative, academic, and student support programs that are responsive to American Indian students. These types of programs will increase the comfort levels of American Indian students as well as the degree to which they identify with the institution and become part of campus academic and social systems (Pavel, 1999). Carrying out the following recommendations will assist institutions in reducing the feelings of anonymity, hostility, and alienation that many American Indians experience in mainstream institutions.

To facilitate a successful transition from high school to college, postsecondary institutions should enter into K–16 partnerships with tribal communities to improve preparation and orientation for college. Such partnerships may result in students having a greater ability to successfully navigate and integrate the social and academic systems on college campuses and improve persistence rates (Pavel, 1999). Summer bridge and orientation programs are examples that may assist students with postsecondary social and academic integration. American Indian K–12 students would benefit greatly from university experiences that enrich their math, science, technology, writing, and reading skills. University faculty also could be used for role models, mentors, and career exploration.

Colleges and universities should be more family-friendly. They could use family involvement to extend the support network for their American Indian students. Organizing family events on campus once or twice per academic year may assist in maintaining the family ties that are so important to the success of American Indian students. In addition, academic institutions can provide technology to maintain communication linkages between students and family members (for example, e-mail, interactive video, newsletters). Moreover, institutions should have child care programs in place to assist those students with children. Students are less likely to miss classes or leave school if they have addressed this basic need in a convenient and satisfactory manner (Stein, 2003).

Colleges and universities should take steps to incorporate American Indian culture into courses, programs, and the architecture and landscape of the campus. Teaching methods that emphasize cooperative learning may be more appropriate for American Indian students who value the family and tribe over individual advancement. Instructional activities and assignments could emphasize group work and cooperation rather than individual competition. In addition to culturally relevant education, mainstream institutions that have established American Indian studies programs and provide a broad range of support services have experienced higher persistence rates for their American Indian students (Wright, 1990).

To incorporate American Indian culture into their landscape, some colleges have built a fire circle, which is a circle of stones with a wood fire in the middle. The circle provides a place for students to pray according to their own tribal beliefs. The belief is that the circle of fire carries the prayers to the heavens. This is an excellent example of an accommodation that mainstream institutions could make for American Indian students that would require a minimum of resources.

Institutions that are geographically close to American Indian communities could form partnerships with tribal colleges and tribal leaders in developing culturally sensitive programming. Faculty members at mainstream universities have specific areas of expertise that could be of value to tribal colleges. Likewise, tribal college personnel have knowledge that will help orient university faculty to life on the reservation.

For such exchanges to occur, institutional commitment is necessary. Campus administrators and leaders must make cultural learning and sensitivity a priority at their institutions. They must encourage and reward faculty for engaging in these activities (Tierney, 1992).

In addition to financial aid and scholarship programs available from federal, state, and tribal governments, institutions should earmark additional financial aid and scholarship support to assist in meeting the unmet financial need of American Indian students (Stein, 2003).

Conclusion

In summary, visions for improving participation and persistence rates for American Indians in higher education will become a reality if institutions provide commitment and leadership, culturally relevant programs, and student support systems, as well as include student perspectives in program planning. Institutions must also continue to collaborate and partner with each other and with tribal nations for the benefit of American Indian students. Inevitably, this will mean additional resources, particularly time and staff for new programs and training and increased financial aid and scholarship funding. Everyone deserves equal access to higher education opportunities, and this should be our goal in supporting American Indian students.

References

American Indian College Fund (AICF). *Cultivating Success: The Critical Value of American Indian Scholarships and the Positive Impact of Tribal College Capital Construction.* Denver, Colo.: AICF, 2003.

American Indian Higher Education Consortium (AIHEC). *Tribal Colleges: An Introduction.* Washington, D.C.: AIHEC, 1999.

Boyer, P. *Native American Colleges: Progress and Prospects.* Princeton, N.J.: Carnegie Foundation for the Advancement of Teaching, 1997.

Low, D. *Touch the Sky.* Lawrence, Kans.: Penthe, 1994.

Martin, R. "Attitudes of Teachers of American Indians Toward Culturally Relevant Education." Doctoral dissertation, University of Kansas, 1994. Abstract in *Dissertation Abstracts International, 56,* 04A.

Matthews, K. "Tribal College Enrollment up 63 Percent." *Community College Week,* 1999, *11*(18), 3.

O'Brien, E. M. "American Indians in Higher Education." *Research Briefs,* 1992, *3*(3), 1–60.

Ortiz, A., and Heavyrunner, I. "Student Access, Retention, and Success: Models of Inclusion and Support." In M.K.P. Benham and W. J. Stein (eds.), *The Renaissance of American Indian Higher Education: Capturing the Dream.* Mahwah, N.J.: Erlbaum, 2003.

Pavel, D. M. *American Indians and Alaska Natives in Higher Education: Research on Participation and Graduation* (ERIC Digest). Charleston, W.Va.: ERIC Clearinghouse on Rural Education and Small Schools, 1992. (ED 348 197)

Pavel, D. M. "American Indians and Alaska Natives in Higher Education: Promoting Access and Achievement." In K. G. Swisher and J. W. Tippeconnic III (eds.), *Next Steps: Research and Practice to Advance Indian Education.* Charleston, W.Va.: ERIC Clearinghouse on Rural Education and Small Schools, 1999.

Stein, W. J. *Tribally Controlled Colleges.* New York: Peter Lang, 1992.

Stein, W. J. "Tribal Colleges: 1968–1998." In K. G. Swisher and J. W. Tippeconnic III (eds.), *Next Steps: Research and Practice to Advance Indian Education.* Charleston, W.Va.: ERIC Clearinghouse on Rural Education and Small Schools, 1999.

Stein, W. J. "Developmental Action for Implementing an Indigenous College: Philosophical Foundations and Pragmatic Steps." In M.K.P. Benham and W. J. Stein (eds.), *The Renaissance of American Indian Higher Education: Capturing the Dream.* Mahwah, N.J.: Erlbaum, 2003.

Tierney, W. G. *Official Encouragement, Institutional Discouragement: Minorities in Academe—The Native American Experience.* Norwood, N.J.: Ablex, 1992.

Wright, B. "American Indian Studies Programs: Surviving the '80s, Thriving in the '90s." *Journal of American Indian Education,* 1990, *30*(1), 17–24.

Wright, B., and Tierney, W. G. "American Indians in Higher Education: A History of Cultural Conflict." *Change,* 1991, *23*(2), 11–20.

DR. ROBERT G. MARTIN (CHEROKEE) *is president of Tohono O'odham Community College and former president of both Haskell Indian Nations University and Southwest Indian Polytechnic Institute.*

This chapter discusses American Indian student services at one university as a model for providing support for Native American students attending a predominantly white institution.

9

American Indian Student Services at UND

Donna L. Brown (Turtle Mountain Chippewa)

Native American student service centers on predominantly white campuses commonly have missions that address academic and social support for Native American students, advocacy on behalf of Native American students, and educational outreach to the campus and local communities. This chapter will describe American Indian Student Services (AISS) at the University of North Dakota (UND) as one model of Native American student support services at a predominantly white institution. The chapter begins by describing the American Indian student population at UND and then AISS at UND. Using the work of Jackson, Smith, and Hill (2003) as a framework, the chapter will then highlight the programs and services that AISS provides. The chapter concludes with recommendations for practice.

American Indian Students at UND

Native Americans have unique needs related to their culture and socio-economic background that necessitate a center of their own. The danger in having one support service center for all ethnic minorities is that the services can be watered down. UND has over four hundred Native American students, the largest minority group in the state and on the campus. North Dakota is home to four American Indian reservations: Turtle Mountain, Spirit Lake, Standing Rock, and Fort Berthold. Therefore, UND has made a special commitment to Native American people across the state and the nation.

Although the numbers of Native Americans attending UND are increasing, the retention of these students remains a concern. For example, after four years at UND, only 4 percent of degree-seeking, first-time, full-time Native American freshmen graduate, as compared to 16 percent of all students. The numbers improve after six years at UND, with 21 percent of Native Americans graduating, but that is still quite low considering that 43 percent of all college students at UND graduate.

The number of students transferring to UND from tribal colleges is increasing. These transfer students are usually more prepared for transition to a four-year institution; however, they still have needs. In addition to having to adjust to a college that is larger and more structured than their home institutions, many Native American transfer students have to overcome cultural differences and juggle family and work responsibilities. Institutions with climates that are not receptive to cultural diversity or supportive of diversity issues create feelings of isolation for many Native American students (Day, 1999).

UND offers a wide array of programs and services designed specifically to assist Native American students at the institution. Among this array are programs and services in the areas of recruitment, admissions, financial aid, housing, orientation, academic support and enhancement, mentorship, advisement, retention, graduation, and alumni activities. Each of these programs and services was designed to address the historical barriers to success in higher education that American Indians have encountered at predominantly white institutions.

AISS at UND

Research findings support the important role of ethnic centers and support services for minorities on predominantly white campuses (Astin, 1993; Day, 1999; Dell, 2000). Furthermore, campuses must ensure that these services and organizations have enough staff, funding, and resources to serve students successfully (Hurtado, Milem, Clayton-Pedersen, and Allen, 1998).

The American Indian Center is located on the edge of the UND campus in a house that was formerly a three-bedroom residence. The house has a kitchen, living room, computer lab, and staff offices. The kitchen is modestly equipped for student needs, and staff members often cook for the students. The staff of eight consists of a director, an assistant director, a learning specialist, a recruiter, two student support advisers, an administrative assistant, and a receptionist.

Institutional funds support AISS's operating expenses and salaries (with the exception of one staff position funded through a federal grant). Most of the other American Indian-related programs at UND are federally funded. Institutional funding for AISS shows commitment for the program from university administration and the state. Another sign of that commitment is the

UND president's recent commitment of $500,000 to build a larger building for the American Indian Center to address increasing Native American student enrollment.

At the American Indian Center, students meet with staff members, study between classes, perhaps take a break and watch a little television, visit with friends, or even get something to eat. AISS tutors staff the building, including the computer lab, Sunday through Thursday evenings and provide walk-in assistance in a wide variety of academic areas. Student organizations commonly host their meetings at the center, and occasionally cultural events and receptions take place there.

Housed in the American Indian Center, AISS focuses on student support. AISS also employs a recruiter who visits Native American communities and schools nationwide. The recruiter frequently coordinates recruitment efforts and activities with the UND office of enrollment services. AISS is a part of the UND's Division of Student Outreach and Services.

Programs and Services

Jackson, Smith, and Hill (2003) give three categories of reasons that Native American college students may not succeed at college: sociocultural factors, academic factors, and personal factors. Sociocultural factors include isolation, lack of accommodation for Native American culture, lack of ethnic identity, various family influences, and lack of or negative interactions with faculty members. Academic factors can include poor high school preparation or possession of a GED. Personal factors that may contribute to nonpersistence include lack of confidence in oneself, low levels of financial support, and stressful family situations such as being a single parent. Support programs that address these barriers are vital in helping Native American students make the transition to and persist in the university setting.

Addressing Sociocultural Factors

AISS offers several programs and services designed to address sociocultural factors that may have an impact on Native American students at UND; this section describes a few of them.

Orientation. Students are highly encouraged to attend UND's new student orientation, but AISS also provides a separate orientation for Native American students. Not a repetition of the UND orientation, it is an opportunity for students to find out about the thirty programs for American Indian students and more importantly to connect with the Native American community at UND.

Social and Cultural Events. AISS offers a variety of social and cultural events throughout the year. The first such event is an annual American Indian-related programs picnic held in the fall. At this event nearly four hundred participants gather, including Native American students, program staff, faculty, and senior university officials (including the president, vice presidents, and deans).

Among the more exciting social opportunities are the presidential leadership luncheons for Native American students. AISS organizes two luncheons per semester, at which staff members cook and serve the meal. The luncheons are small (approximately twenty students participate) to give the university's president an opportunity to have intimate, one-on-one conversations with the students.

Student Organizations. UND has six student organizations for Native American students. The largest is the UND Indian Association (UNDIA). UNDIA is open to all Native American students attending UND, and several non-Indian students also participate. Meetings and activities occur throughout the year, but the premier event is the UNDIA Time-out and Wacipi, occurring the first weekend in April. Time-out is a week of presentations, speakers, and films on a theme chosen by the year's executive committee. Past themes have focused on health, tribal sovereignty, and environmental preservation. The week culminates with a three-day powwow called the Wacipi. The Wacipi, which brings together approximately three thousand people, is a contest powwow that draws over seven hundred dancers and about twenty-five drum groups. In addition to providing this important opportunity for social interaction for the students, UNDIA invites the community to watch, participate, and learn about Native American people and culture.

The other five organizations are focused on particular career fields: law, health careers, journalism and communications, business, and engineering. Some AISS staff members serve as official advisers to these organizations, and others sometimes advise unofficially. UND highly encourages students to participate in at least one student organization as yet another opportunity for social interaction.

Addressing Academic Factors

AISS also offers several programs and services designed to address academic factors.

Tutoring. AISS employs five students as tutors each semester. Although it is desirable to attract Native Americans for these positions, it is more important to cover a wide variety of academic areas to address the students' needs. Currently, AISS employs two Native American and three non-Native tutors. This diverse group provides walk-in assistance for five hours five evenings per week, Sunday through Thursday. AISS hires and schedules the tutors to provide assistance in a wide variety of course work each semester. The tutors double as overseers for the American Indian Center and computer lab, providing computer and Internet assistance when necessary. The computer lab is equipped with eight computers and two laser printers. Discs, paper, and other supplies are also provided for students. These services are free of charge, and no appointments are necessary.

Retention Program. AISS has implemented a retention program that students monitor themselves. Anyone can participate, but the program is designed with freshman and sophomore students in mind. Requirements include visiting with AISS staff twice per semester at a minimum, participating in orientation, attending at least one social or cultural event, meeting with each of their instructors once per semester, and meeting with their assigned adviser from their college before registering for the following semester. Benefits include improved academic performance, ongoing encouragement and advisement, priority registration, and early notification of scholarships and other opportunities.

Soup on Friday. On Fridays the American Indian Center serves soup without charge over the noon hour. The goal of this program is to help keep the students on campus through Friday's courses, as many students travel home to their reservation communities on weekends. Especially through the North Dakota winter months, many students find a free bowl of hot soup most welcome.

Addressing Personal Factors

In addition, AISS offers programs and services designed to address personal factors.

Application Processes. One of the first barriers to college that many Native American students encounter is not having enough money to apply for both admission to UND and housing. AISS has an agreement with Undergraduate Admissions to defer fees if the applicant is unable to pay at the time of application. After discussions with the potential student, an AISS staff member determines whether or not the student needs this service. If so, the staff member provides a letter, along with the student's application, requesting a deferment. The student is able to be admitted and in turn apply for scholarships, housing, and so on. The student must pay the fee when he or she receives financial aid.

Because many of the students at UND are either married, married with children, or single parents, they are in need of family housing. The waiting list for family housing can be lengthy, often requiring students to be on the list for up to a year. To be put on the waiting list, one has to submit a fee along with the housing application. Potential students who do not have the fee can request a deferment through AISS, which enables them to get on the housing waiting list as soon as possible. This allows students to have some choice in the apartment they get assigned to. In the past a student who did not have the money for the deposit typically waited for financial aid disbursement and either had to wait for appropriate housing or be placed in an apartment that did not meet his or her needs. For this and the following housing assistance, AISS proposed and initiated programs to address the needs of Native Americans; the programs are open to all students applying to UND.

Students requesting housing in residence halls face a similar barrier. When students are assigned to a residence hall, they must submit $200 to hold their room assignment. UND makes assignments according to students' preferences; if they apply early, they often get their first choice along with their choice of roommate. Once assigned, the student must pay the fee within two weeks or give up the first-choice assignment. Often Native American students do not have the money. They can apply for a reduced deposit and, depending on individual circumstances, may pay as little as $25.

Financial Aid and Scholarship Assistance. AISS staff members often assist students in filling out the Free Application for Federal Student Aid (FAFSA) because many of them are first-generation college students whose family members can provide little guidance through the application process. In addition, AISS keeps a scholarship bank up-to-date with current scholarship opportunities. After discussing a student's academic interests with the individual, AISS staff are able to provide students with scholarship applications that fit their needs. Staff will go so far as to review a student's scholarship essay, making recommendations for content, flow, and grammar. They also frequently provide letters of recommendation.

UND has a cultural diversity tuition waiver program, which AISS proposed and initiated. Rather than requesting a waiver program for Native American students only, AISS proposed a cultural diversity tuition waiver program to allow all students the opportunity to benefit from interactions with and experiences of other cultures. Presently 159 students are receiving waivers, with ninety of those waivers going to Native Americans. With over four hundred Native Americans attending UND, it is obvious that there are not enough waivers to provide all Native American students with one. The Student Financial Aid office administers the cultural diversity tuition waiver program, and an AISS staff member serves on the advisory board to provide input on key programmatic decisions. Students must apply by a set deadline each year and face strong competition for the waivers. A student who receives a waiver must meet academic standards designated by the board to continue receiving the waiver.

Often a student's financial aid disbursement is delayed for a variety of reasons, among them verification, budget appeal, or the need for additional documentation to complete a file. AISS staff assist students in identifying and resolving the problems so that the students do not end up paying late fees or being dropped from their classes because they have not paid tuition.

Recommendations

Following are some recommendations for those who have significant numbers of Native Americans on their campus and who are fortunate enough to have an American Indian Center:

Organize a Native American advisory group to address education, personal, social, and cultural needs.

Establish quality working relationships with American Indian high schools, tribal colleges, and other organizations to enhance recruitment and retention efforts.

Encourage faculty to serve as mentors for Native American students.

Promote a variety of educational and cultural programs that send the message that Native American students are welcome and an important constituency on the campus.

Following are some recommendations for those who do not have a significant population of Native Americans on their campus but strive to improve the retention of Native Americans:

Assign someone (faculty or staff member) the responsibility of assessing the needs of Native American students and to serve as a mentor for them.

Develop an academic enhancement program for Native Americans, who will come to campus with a variety of skill levels. This should consist of advisement, academic assessment, tutoring, study skills workshops, writing assistance, and mentoring.

Remember that you cannot treat all students equally. Accommodations are not only warranted, they are just. Therefore, to provide activities and opportunities for Native American students is not to give them an advantage over other students; rather, such programs and services are a means to get Native American students on the same playing field.

Conclusion

Having a place where Native American students feel like they belong and feel comfortable is extremely important to their success in higher education. Students usually have family that is far away, so having a welcoming home away from home is critical. In addition, colleges should provide adequate staff at these centers to provide assistance, encouragement, and advisement on demand. Additionally, incoming students need to be informed and motivated to use these and all the academic support services that the university provides.

It is our hope that students will eventually be able to be weaned off some of the services mentioned in this chapter. For example, once an AISS staff member has assisted a student with the FAFSA, we hope that he or she may be able to fill it out without help the following year. Once a counselor has assisted the student a number of times, we hope that the student can accept the responsibility of resolving similar issues on his or her own. AISS works to empower students, build independence and leadership skills, and encourage persistence through to graduation. AISS staff strive to build stronger American Indian communities across the state and nation, one successful student at a time.

References

Astin, A. W. *What Matters in College: Four Critical Years Revisited.* San Francisco: Jossey-Bass, 1993.

Day, D. R. "Perceptions of American Indian Students of Their Experiences and Factors Related to Retention in Selected Institutions of Higher Education." Doctoral dissertation, University of North Dakota, 1999. Abstract in *Dissertation Abstracts International, 60,* 06A.

Dell, C. A. "The First Semester Experiences of American Indian Transfer Students." Doctoral dissertation, Montana State University, 2000. Abstract in *Dissertation Abstracts International, 61,* 02A.

Hurtado, S., Milem, J. F., Clayton-Pedersen, A. R., and Allen, W. R. "Enhancing Campus Climates for Racial/Ethnic Diversity: Educational Policy and Practice." *Review of Higher Education,* 1998, 21(3), 279–302.

Jackson, A. P., Smith, S. A., and Hill, C. L. "Academic Persistence Among Native American College Students." *Journal of College Student Development,* 2003, 44(4), 548–565.

DR. DONNA L. BROWN (TURTLE MOUNTAIN CHIPPEWA) *is assistant director of American Indian student services at the University of North Dakota.*

10

This chapter describes nine of this volume's themes and offers summary recommendations stemming from those themes.

From Discussion to Action

George S. McClellan, Mary Jo Tippeconnic Fox (Comanche), and Shelly C. Lowe (Navajo)

Although this volume's authors are a diverse group and speak with unique voices, readers will have detected a number of common themes running throughout the previous chapters. Stemming from those nine themes are the following summary recommendations for better serving and supporting Native American students in higher education.

One of the themes throughout the volume is the lack of knowledge among professionals in higher education about Native Americans. Not only harmful to Native American students, parents, and nations, the lack of knowledge is harmful to non-Natives in a variety of ways. Similarly, the lack of knowledge about Native American higher education and Native American students, staff, and faculty has a negative effect on the experiences and success of these members of our campus communities as well as on our campus communities themselves. Professionals in higher education must seek to gain greater knowledge about Native American history, culture, and contemporary issues, as well as the experiences of Native American students, staff, and faculty. In seeking this knowledge, professionals should turn to Native American sources wherever possible.

Both Native and non-Native professional associations can play an important role in assisting higher education professionals to develop the additional knowledge. Native American education associations such as the National Indian Education Association should seek to build greater emphasis internally on higher education, and Native American and non-Native professionals in higher education should take advantage of the resources available through membership and participation in Native

American education professional associations (a partial list of these associations is available in the Resources section of this volume). Non-Native professional associations (including the American Association for Higher Education, American College Personnel Association, Association for the Study of Higher Education, and National Association for Student Affairs Professionals) should focus on establishing relationships with Native American education associations, recruiting more Native American professionals into higher education and into the ranks of their membership, and in supporting the dissemination of best practices in Native American higher education.

The diversity of Native American people and Native American experiences is a second theme. It can be convenient, and in some cases appropriate, to discuss Native Americans as a group. However, professionals in higher education must keep in mind that there are distinct differences among tribal affiliations, tribal cultures, senses of Native American identity, and experiential backgrounds (including whether someone is from a reservation, nonreservation rural, or urban environment) that are important to consider when working with Native American people.

A third theme, tribal sovereignty, runs rich and strong throughout the chapters in this volume. Professionals in higher education must understand and accept tribal sovereignty as an elemental component of their work with Native American students, staff, faculty, and tribal nations.

A fourth theme is that the use of Euro-American theories, models, and practices is inappropriate and inadequate when working with Native American people. Professionals need to become aware of and make use of indigenous theories, models, and practices in seeking to serve and support the success of Native American students, staff, and faculty.

The need for an intentional and coordinated focus in higher education on improving the rates of participation and persistence to graduation for Native American students is a fifth theme. A critical component in achieving the goal of increasing these rates is to recognize and act on the knowledge that supporting the success of Native American students in higher education must begin long before those students arrive on campus. Designating an individual or office to have the primary responsibility for supporting the success of Native American students is an important step, but the work must be a responsibility shared by all departments on campus. Although additional research and scholarship would be beneficial, the extant literature provides a useful foundation with which to begin enhancing efforts to improve participation and retention of Native American students. Some of the emerging indigenous approaches to increasing Native American participation and persistence offer particular promise as frameworks for this work.

A sixth theme is the need to consider the impact of existing procedures, policies, and practices on Native American students. Professionals in higher education should strive for clarity and transparency in communicating important information to Native American students, families, and leaders. Wherever possible, we strongly advise flexibility regarding fees and forms so that cultural differences and financial disadvantages do not become barriers to higher education.

A seventh theme is the need in higher education to recruit, retain, and promote Native American staff and faculty. Doing so requires a commitment on the part of professionals and institutions to be proactive in their outreach and more inclusive in the kinds of credentials and experiences that they value in the hiring and promotion processes.

An eighth theme in the volume is the need for additional research in almost all aspects of Native American higher education. Native American and non-Native scholars must engage in exploring the important unanswered questions regarding the experiences of Native American students, staff, and faculty on our campuses. Native American and non-Native scholars must assess Native American students' usage and satisfaction with programs and services; the impact of campus programs and services on Native American experiences and success; and the campus climate for Native American students, staff, and faculty. Scholars must conduct research and assessment regarding all of these issues in ways that are culturally appropriate and respectful of tribal sovereignty. Faircloth and Tippeconnic (2004) offer an excellent listing of literature that can be helpful to researchers striving to conduct research that makes use of and is respectful of indigenous knowledge and communities.

A ninth theme, and perhaps the most important, is that it is essential for Native American people to be involved in every aspect of improving Native American higher education. There can be no doubt that the time has come to recognize and respond in as many ways as possible to the observation that what is missing from Native American education is Native Americans (Deloria and Wildcat, 2001). Native American students, staff, faculty, parents, leaders, elders, alumni, and others must be present, heard, and honored through action in any deliberations and decisions affecting the future of Native American higher education.

Although these nine themes are evidence that this volume covers a great deal of material, the limitations of time, resources, and words have nonetheless shaped this volume in important ways. The focus throughout is on Native American higher education in the United States. We were not able to address important issues such as indigenous education in other countries, changes in Native American population demographics that have implications for K–16 education, colleges and universities' use of Native American mascots or logos, or the impact of tribal economic development (including the emergence of tribal gaming) on Native American education.

We hope that this volume has informed, challenged, and inspired its readers regarding working with Native American students in higher education. In closing, we offer one final recommendation. If we are to achieve what is possible in serving and supporting Native American students in higher education, we must now move from discussion to action.

References

Deloria, V., Jr., and Wildcat, D. R. *Power and Place: Indian Education in America.* Golden, Colo.: Fulcrum Resources, 2001.
Faircloth, S. C., and Tippeconnic, J. W., III. "Resource Guide: Utilizing Research Methods That Respect and Empower Indigenous Knowledge." *Tribal College Journal,* 2004, *16*(2), 24–29.

DR. GEORGE S. MCCLELLAN is vice president for student development at Dickinson State University.

DR. MARY JO TIPPECONNIC FOX (COMANCHE) is chair of the American Indian studies programs and ambassador to the Indian nations at the University of Arizona.

SHELLY C. LOWE (NAVAJO) is a doctoral candidate in higher education at the University of Arizona.

RESOURCES

Books

Benham, M.K.P., and Stein, W. J. (eds.). *The Renaissance of American Indian Higher Education: Capturing the Dream.* Mahwah, N.J.: Erlbaum, 2003.

Boyer, P. *Native American Colleges: Progress and Prospects.* Princeton, N.J.: Carnegie Foundation for the Advancement of Teaching, 1997.

Carney, C. M. *Native American Higher Education in the United States.* New Brunswick, N.J.: Transaction, 1999.

Deloria, V., Jr., and Wildcat, D. R. *Power and Place: Indian Education in America.* Golden, Colo.: Fulcrum Resources, 2001.

Sherkoff, M. M. *Dream Catchers: A Transfer Guide for Native American College Students with Special Assistance for Those from Tribal Colleges.* Irvine: University of California, 1991.

Swisher, K. G., and Tippeconnic, J. W., III (eds.). *Next Steps: Research and Practice to Advance Indian Education.* Charleston, W.V.: ERIC Clearinghouse on Rural Education and Small Schools, 1999.

Szasz, M. C. *Education and the American Indian: The Road to Self-Determination Since 1928.* (3rd ed.) Albuquerque: University of New Mexico Press, 1999.

Tierney, W. G. *Official Encouragement, Institutional Discouragement: Minorities in Academe—The Native American Experience.* Norwood, N.J.: Ablex, 1992.

Periodicals

Journal of American Indian Education
Center for Indian Education
Arizona State University
P.O. Box 871311
Tempe, AZ 85287–1311
http://jaie.asu.edu

Tribal College Journal of American Indian Higher Education
P.O. Box 720
Mancos, CO 81328
970–533–9170 Voice
970–533–9145 Fax
http://www.tribalcollegejournal.org

Organizations

American Indian College Fund (http://www.collegefund.org) offers scholarships for American Indian college students and supports tribally controlled colleges and universities.

American Indian Graduate Center (http://www.aigc.com) works to improve the cultural and economic well-being of American Indians and Native Alaskans, individually and tribally, through graduate education.

American Indian Higher Education Consortium (http://www.aihec.org) supports tribally controlled colleges and the national movement for tribal self-determination through the pursuit of four objectives: maintaining commonly held standards of quality in American Indian education, supporting the development of new tribally controlled colleges, promoting and assisting in the development of legislation to support American Indian higher education, and encouraging greater participation by American Indians in the development of higher education policy.

American Indian Science and Engineering Society (AISES)— (http://www.aises.org) nurtures community by bridging science and technology with traditional Native American values. Through its educational programs, AISES provides opportunities for American Indians and Native Alaskans to pursue studies in science, engineering, and technology.

First Nations Adult and Higher Education Consortium (http://www. fnahec.org) promotes unity and cooperative action in the development of postsecondary educational institutions controlled by First Nations.

National Indian Education Association (http://www.niea.org) supports traditional Native American cultures and values, enables Native American learners to become contributing members of their communities, promotes Native American control of educational institutions, and improves educational opportunities and resources for American Indians, Alaska Natives, and Native Hawaiians throughout the United States.

Tribally Controlled Colleges and Universities

This list comes from the American Indian Higher Education Consortium Web site (http://www.aihec.org/CollegeRoster.html) and was current as of December 2004.

Bay Mills Community College (Bay
   Mills Indian Community)
12214 West Lake Shore Drive
Brimley, MI 49715
906–248–3354 Voice
906–248–3351 Fax
http://www.bmcc.org

Blackfeet Community College
   (Blackfeet)
P.O. Box 819
Browning, MT 59417
406–338–7755 Voice
406–338–3272 Fax
http://www.bfcc.org

Cankdeska Cikana Community
   College (Spirit Lake Sioux)
P.O. Box 269
Fort Totten, ND 58335
701–766–4415 Voice
701–766–4077 Fax
http://www.littlehoop.cc

Chief Dull Knife College (Northern
   Cheyenne)
P.O. Box 98
Lame Deer, MT 59043
406–477–6215 Voice
406–477–6219 Fax
http://www.cdkc.edu

College of Menominee Nation
   (Menominee)
P.O. Box 1179
Keshena, WI 54135
715–799–4921 Voice
715–799–1308 Fax
http://www.menominee.edu

Crownpoint Institute of
   Technology (Navajo)
P.O. Box 849
Crownpoint, NM 87313
505–786–4100 Voice
505–786–5644 Fax
http://crownpointtech.org

D-Q University (Private institution
   governed by Indian Board of
   Trustees)
P.O. Box 409
Davis, CA 95617
530–758–0470 Voice
530–758–4891 Fax
http://www.dqu.cc.ca.us

Diné College (Navajo)
P.O. Box 126
Tsaile, AZ 86556
928–724–6669 Voice
928–724–3327 Fax
http://www.dinecollege.edu

Fond du Lac Tribal and
Community College (Jointly governed by the Fond du Lac and the
State of Minnesota)
2101 14th Street
Cloquet, MN 55720–2964
218–879–0800 Voice
218–879–0814 Fax
http://www.fdltcc.edu

Fort Belknap College (Gros Ventre
and Assiniboine)
P.O. Box 159
Harlem, MT 59526
406–353–2607 Voice
406–353–2898 Fax
http://www.fbcc.edu

Fort Berthold Community College
(Three Affiliated Tribes)
P.O. Box 490
New Town, ND 58763
701–627–4738 Voice
701–627–3609 Fax
http://www.fbcc.bia.edu

Fort Peck Community College
(Fort Peck Assiniboine and
Sioux)
P.O. Box 398
Poplar, MT 59255
406–768–5551 Voice
406–768–5552 Fax
http://www.fpcc.edu

Haskell Indian Nations University
(BIA)
155 Indian Avenue, Box 5030
Lawrence, KS 66046–4800
785–749–8404 Voice
785–749–8411 Fax
http://www.haskell.edu/haskell

Institute of American Indian Arts
(BIA)

83 Avan Nu Po Road
Santa Fe, NM 87505
505–424–2300 Voice
505–424–0050 Fax
http://www.iaiancad.org

Keweenaw Bay Ojibwa Community
College (Keweenaw Bay
Ojibwa)
409 Superior Avenue
P.O. Box 519
Baraga, MI 49908
906–353–8161 Voice
906–353–8107 Fax
http://www.kbocc.org

Lac Courte Oreilles Ojibwa
Community College (Lac Courte
Oreilles Ojibwa)
13466 West Trepania Road
Hayward, WI 54843
715–634–4790 Voice
715–634–5049 Fax
http://www.lco-college.edu

Leech Lake Tribal College (Leech
Lake Ojibwa)
Route 3, Box 100
Cass Lake, MN 56633
218–335–4200 Voice
218–335–4209 Fax
http://www.lltc.org

Little Big Horn College (Crow)
P.O. Box 370
Crow Agency, MT 59022
406–638–3100 Voice
406–638–3169 Fax
http://www.lbhc.cc.mt.us

Little Priest Tribal College
(Winnebago)
P.O. Box 270
Winnebago, NE 68071
402–878–2380 Voice

402–878–2355 Fax
http://www.lptc.bia.edu

Nebraska Indian Community
College (Omaha, Santee Sioux,
and Winnebago)
College Hill
P.O. Box 428
Macy, NE 68039
402–837–5078 Voice
402–837–4183 Fax
http://www.thenicc.edu

Northwest Indian College (Lummi)
2522 Kwina Road
Bellingham, WA 98226
360–676–2772 Voice
360–738–0136 Fax
http://www.nwic.edu

Oglala Lakota College (Oglala
Lakota)
490 Piya Wiconi Road
Kyle, SD 57752
605–455–6022 Voice
605–455–60236 Fax
http://www.olc.edu

Red Crow Community College
(Blood)
P.O. Box 1258
Cardston, Alberta
Canada T0K 0K0
403–737–2400 Voice
403–737–2101 Fax
http://www.redcrowcollege.com

Saginaw Chippewa Tribal College
(Saginaw Chippewa)
2284 Enterprise Drive
Mount Pleasant, MI 48858
989–775–4123 Voice
989–775–4528 Fax
http://www.sagchip.org/tribal
college

Salish Kootenai College (Salish and
Kootenai)
P.O. Box 117
Pablo, MT 59855
406–275–4800 Voice
406–275–4801 Fax
http://www.skc.edu

Sinte Gleska University (Sicangu
Lakota)
P.O. Box 490
Rosebud, SD 57570
605–747–2263 Voice
605–747–2098 Fax
http://www.sinte.edu

Sisseton Wahpeton Community
College (Sisseton Wahpeton
Sioux)
P.O. Box 689
Sisseton, SD 57262
605–698–3966 Voice
605–698–3132 Fax
http://www.swc.tc

Si Tanka University (Cheyenne
River Sioux)
P.O. Box 220
Eagle Butte, SD 57625
605–964–6044 Voice
605–964–1144 Fax
http://www.sitanka.edu

Sitting Bull College (Standing Rock
Sioux)
1341–92nd Street
Fort Yates, ND 58538
701–854–3861 Voice
701–854–3403 Fax
http://www.sittingbull.edu

Southwestern Indian Polytechnic
Institute (BIA)
P.O. Box 10146
Albuquerque, NM 87184

505–346–2347 Voice
505–346–2343 Fax
http://www.sipi.bia.edu

Stone Child College (Chippewa-
 Cree)
RR1, Box 1082
Box Elder, MT 59521
406–395–4313 Voice
406–395–4836 Fax
http://www.montana.edu/wwwscc

Tohono O'odham Community
 College (Tohono O'odham)
P.O. Box 3129
Sells, AZ 85634
520–383–8401 Voice
520–383–8403 Fax
http://www.tocc.cc.az.us

Turtle Mountain Community
 College (Turtle Mountain
 Chippewa)
P.O. Box 340
Belcourt, ND 58316

701–477–7862 Voice
701–477–7807 Fax
http://www.tm.edu

United Tribes Technical College
 (Three Affiliated Tribes, Spirit
 Lake Sioux, Sisseton Wahpeton
 Sioux, Standing Rock Sioux,
 and Turtle Mountain
 Chippewa)
3315 University Drive
Bismarck, ND 58504
701–255–3285 Voice
701–530–0605 Fax
http://www.uttc.edu

White Earth Tribal and
 Community College (White
 Earth Chippewa)
210 Main Street South
P.O. Box 478
Mahnomen, MN 56557
218–935–0417 Voice
218–953–0423 Fax
http://www.wetcc.org

INDEX

Academic integration, 20, 82
Affective foundation, of education, 75
AICF. *See* American Indian College Fund (AICF)
AIHEC. *See* American Indian Higher Education Consortium (AIHEC)
Aitken, L. P., 18, 22, 23, 51, 54
Alaska Natives, 23
Alawiye, O., 42
Allen, W. R., 88
Almeida, D. A., 22
American Council on Education, 18
American Indian College, 12, 13
American Indian College Fund (AICF), 80, 82, 100
American Indian descriptor, 62
American Indian Higher Education Consortium (AIHEC), 8, 9, 10, 11, 13, 80, 81, 100
American Indian Science and Engineering Society, 100
American Indian students. *See* Native American students
Application process, 91–92
Architecture, 82, 85
Artistic foundation, of education, 74–75
Assimilation: in colonial era, 9; and cultural identity, 20–21
Astin, A. W., 18, 88
Attrition, 17
Austin, R. D., 3, 41

Bacone College, 13
Banks, S. R., 46
Barnhardt, R., 26, 54
Barr, M. J., 3
Beaty, C. K., 20, 23
Beaty, J., 20, 23
Belgarde, W. L., 8, 9, 10, 11, 12, 19, 21, 23
Benedict, J., 64
Benjamin, D., 17, 18, 19, 21
Bergstrom, A., 51
Biemer, P., 18, 21
Blimling, G., 50
Boutwell, R. C., 20
Boyer, P., 10, 11, 12, 17, 19, 22, 46, 80, 81
Brady, J. V., 44

Braxton, J. M., 27
Brokenleg, M., 21
Brown, D. L., 4, 20, 87
Brown, L. L., 17, 19, 23, 50
Buckley, A., 22
Burr, P. L., 24
Burr, R. M., 24

Cabrera, V. A., 8
Cain, C. L., 19, 20
Cajete, G. A., 4, 69, 70, 73, 74
Carney, C. M., 7, 8, 9, 10, 11, 12, 13, 17, 23–24
Carroll, R. E., 20
Castellanos, J., 19, 20
Ceremonial practices, 72
Certificate of Indian Blood, 64, 68n.3
Chambers, S., 17, 18, 19, 20, 21, 23
Choctaw Nation, 9
Cibik, M. A., 20, 23
Clark, A. S., 19
Clayton-Pedersen, A. R., 88
Cleary, L. M., 51
Cohen, F. S., 67n.1
Cole, J. S., 19, 20
College of William and Mary, 8
Colonial era, of Native American higher education, 8–9
Colonialism, 66
Communal foundation, of education, 75–76
Cook-Lynn, E., 52
Cooper, J., 23
Cooperative learning, 85
Corbine, J. L., 21
Counseling, 21
Cranney, G., 23
Croaton Normal School, 9–10
Cross, W. T., 52
Crowson, R. L., 22
Cultural events, 89–90
Cultural identity, 20–21, 38–39; and cultural change, 64–65; and ethnic nomenclature, 62; and legal and political status, 63–64; and multiethnic makeup, 66; overview of, 61–62; personal nature of, 65; and racial attitudes, 62–63
Cultural revitalization, 47

105

Tribally controlled colleges: benefits of, 46, 80; challenges of, 12–13; and culturally relevant education, 82–85; degrees offered by, 11–12; emergence of, 11–12; enrollment in, 81; funding of, 12–13, 80–81; graduation rates in, 12; list of, 101–104; non-Native colleges' partnership with, 46; number of, 80; organization of, 80–81; overview of, 79–80; recommendations for, 84–86; retention in, 22; role of, 12; students in, 81–82
Tribally Controlled Community College Act (1978), 11
Trust, 26
Tuition waiver programs, 92
Turner, S., 26
Tutoring, 90

United States Office of Education, 20
University of Kansas, 83
University of North Carolina, Pembroke, 10

University of North Dakota (UND), 87–93
University of Tulsa, 9

Verdugo, R. R., 52
Vision Quest course, 83
Visionary foundation, of education, 74
Vocational training, 10

Waters, A., 69
Wato, 82
Western values, 46 47
White privilege, 62–63
Whitehorse, D. M., 21
Wijeyesinghe, C. L., 66
Wildcat, D. R., 69, 97
Williams, K., 20
Wilson, P., 49
Wolfle, L. M., 23
Wood, M., 73
Woodcock, D. B., 42
World War II, 11
Wright, B., 8, 18, 19, 21, 22, 23, 85
Wright, D. J., 26

Back Issue/Subscription Order Form

Copy or detach and send to:
Jossey-Bass, A Wiley Imprint, 989 Market Street, San Francisco CA, 94103-1741

Call or fax toll-free: Phone 888-378-2537 6:30AM – 3PM PST; Fax 888-481-2665

Back Issues: Please send me the following issues at $27 each
(Important: please include ISBN number with your order.)

_____

_____

_____

$ _____   Total for single issues

$ _____   SHIPPING CHARGES: SURFACE   Domestic Canadian
First Item $5.00 $6.00
Each Add'l Item $3.00 $1.50
For next-day and second-day delivery rates, call the number listed above.

Subscriptions   Please __ start __ renew my subscription to *New Directions for Student Services* for the year 2_____at the following rate:

U.S.	__ Individual $75	__ Institutional $170
Canada	__ Individual $75	__ Institutional $210
All Others	__ Individual $99	__ Institutional $244

**For more information about online subscriptions visit
www.wileyinterscience.com**

$ _____   Total single issues and subscriptions (Add appropriate sales tax for your state for single issue orders. No sales tax for U.S. subscriptions. Canadian residents, add GST for subscriptions and single issues.)

__Payment enclosed (U.S. check or money order only)

__VISA __ MC __ AmEx Card #_____Exp.Date_____

Signature _____ Day Phone _____

__Bill Me (U.S. institutional orders only. Purchase order required.)

Purchase order # _____
Federal Tax ID13559302   **GST 89102 8052**

Name _____

Address _____

_____

Phone _____ E-mail _____

For more information about Jossey-Bass, visit our Web site at www.josseybass.com

SS103   **Contemporary Financial Issues in Student Affairs**
John H. Schuh
This volume addresses the challenging financial situation facing higher
education and offers creative solutions for student affairs staff. Topics
include the differences between public and private institutions in funding
student activities, how to demonstrate financial accountability to
stakeholders, plus ways to address budget challenges in student unions,
health centers, campus recreation, counseling centers, and student housing.
ISBN: 0-7879-7173-1

SS102   **Meeting the Special Needs of Adult Students**
Deborah Kilgore, Penny J. Rice
This volume examines the ways student services professionals can best help
adult learners. Chapters highlight the specific challenges that adult
enrollment brings to traditional four-year and postgraduate institutions,
which are often focused on the traditional-aged student experience.
Explaining that adult students are typically involved in campus life in
different ways than younger students are, the volume provides student
services professionals with good guidance on serving an ever-growing
population.
ISBN: 0-7879-6991-5

SS101   **Planning and Achieving Successful Student Affairs Facilities Projects**
Jerry Price
Provides student affairs professionals with an examination of critical
facilities issues by exploring the experiences of their colleagues. Illustrates
that students' educational experiences are affected by residence halls,
student unions, dining services, recreation and wellness centers, and campus
grounds, and that student affairs professionals make valuable contributions
to the success of campus facility projects. Covers planning, budgeting,
collaboration, and communication through case studies and lessons learned.
ISBN: 0-7879-6847-1

SS100   **Student Affairs and External Relations**
Mary Beth Snyder
Building positive relations with external constituents is as important in
student affairs work as it is in any other university or college division. This
issue is a long-overdue resource of ideas, strategies, and information aimed
at making student affairs leaders more effective in their interactions with
important off-campus partners, supporters, and agencies. Chapter authors
explore the current challenges facing the student services profession as well
as the emerging opportunities worthy of student affairs interest.
ISBN: 0-7879-6342-9

SS99   **Addressing Contemporary Campus Safety Issues**
Christine K. Wilkinson, James A. Rund
Provided for practitioners as a resource book for both historical and evolving
issues, this guide covers hazing, parental partnerships, and collaborative
relationships between universities and the neighboring community.
Addressing a new definition of a safe campus environment, the editors have
identified topics such as the growth in study abroad, the implications of
increased usage of technology on campus, and campus response to
September 11. In addition, large-scale crisis responses to student riots and
multiple campus tragedies have been described in case studies. The issue
speaks to a more contemporary definition of a safe campus environment that

addresses not only physical safety issues but also those of a psychological nature, a more diverse student body, and quality of life.
ISBN: 0-7879-6341-0

SS98   **The Art and Practical Wisdom of Student Affairs Leadership**
Jon Dalton, Marguerite McClinton
This issue collects reflections, stories, and advice about the art and practice of student affairs leadership. Ten senior student affairs leaders were asked to maintain a journal and record their personal reflections on practical wisdom they have gained in the profession. The authors looked inside themselves to provide personal and candid insight into the convictions and values that have guided them in their work and lives.
ISBN: 0-7879-6340-2

SS97   **Working with Asian American College Students**
Marylu K. McEwen, Corinne Maekawa Kodama, Alvin N. Alvarez, Sunny Lee, Christopher T. H. Liang
Highlights the diversity of Asian American college students, analyzes the "model minority" myth and the stereotype of the "perfidious foreigner," and points out the need to consider the racial identity and racial consciousness of Asian American students. Various authors propose a model of Asian American student development, address issues of Asian Americans who are at educational risk, discuss the importance of integration and collaboration between student affairs and Asian American studies programs, and offer strategies for developing socially conscious Asian American student leaders.
ISBN: 0-7879-6292-9S

**NEW DIRECTIONS FOR STUDENT SERVICES
IS NOW AVAILABLE ONLINE AT WILEY INTERSCIENCE**

What is Wiley InterScience?

Wiley InterScience is the dynamic online content service from John Wiley & Sons delivering the full text of over 300 leading scientific, technical, medical, and professional journals, plus major reference works, the acclaimed *Current Protocols* laboratory manuals, and even the full text of select Wiley print books online.

What are some special features of Wiley InterScience?

Wiley InterScience Alerts is a service that delivers table of contents via e-mail for any journal available on Wiley InterScience as soon as a new issue is published online.
Early View is Wiley's exclusive service presenting individual articles online as soon as they are ready, even before the release of the compiled print issue. These articles are complete, peer-reviewed, and citable.
CrossRef is the innovative multi-publisher reference linking system enabling readers to move seamlessly from a reference in a journal article to the cited publication, typically located on a different server and published by a different publisher.

How can I access Wiley InterScience?

Visit http://www.interscience.wiley.com

Guest Users can browse Wiley InterScience for unrestricted access to journal Tables of Contents and Article Abstracts, or use the powerful search engine.
Registered Users are provided with a *Personal Home Page* to store and manage customized alerts, searches, and links to favorite journals and articles. Additionally, Registered Users can view free Online Sample Issues and preview selected material from major reference works.
Licensed Customers are entitled to access full-text journal articles in PDF, with select journals also offering full-text HTML.

How do I become an Authorized User?

Authorized Users are individuals authorized by a paying Customer to have access to the journals in Wiley InterScience. For example, a university that subscribes to Wiley journals is considered to be the Customer. Faculty, staff and students authorized by the university to have access to those journals in Wiley InterScience are Authorized Users. Users should contact their Library for information on which Wiley journals they have access to in Wiley InterScience.

ASK YOUR INSTITUTION ABOUT WILEY INTERSCIENCE TODAY!

Printed in the United States
123744LV00002B/160/A